MANIFESTO

A book about the end of traditional media? A little ironic, perhaps. This is how it happened.

I started working with the Internet when I finished high school in 1994. In that same year, Netscape Navigator, the first commercial web browser, became available, signalling the birth of a new era. In the heady days that followed, the world was consumed by dotcom fever and I was part of it – running an Internet start-up, setting up a digital research agency and even working in strategy for a major media company. If you were part of that early vanguard, explaining what you did was never easy. I found this especially true when it came to my family; I knew they secretly hoped that I would give up this madness and become a banker or a lawyer. But try as I might, the World Wide Web was like an inescapable centre of gravity. The more I realized its future potential, the further it drew me in.

It was while working in Asia over the last few years that my eyes were finally opened to what was coming. Here, subway commuters were already watching television on tiny handsets, teenagers were becoming addicted to gaming in virtual worlds, bestselling novels were being composed entirely on mobile phones, and the success of a new generation of pop stars was fluctuating in step with fickle tastes in ringtones and digital merchandise.

Suddenly, I realized that the future was not simply about producing the next shiny gadget; our whole relationship with technology was changing. People were becoming more connected, more networked. Entertainment would never be the same again.

Digital distribution was taking all the familiar formats of media, such as music, movies, television and games, and turning them into something more fluid, something that consumers could play with – and that's exactly what they would go on to do.

This book is about what happens next.

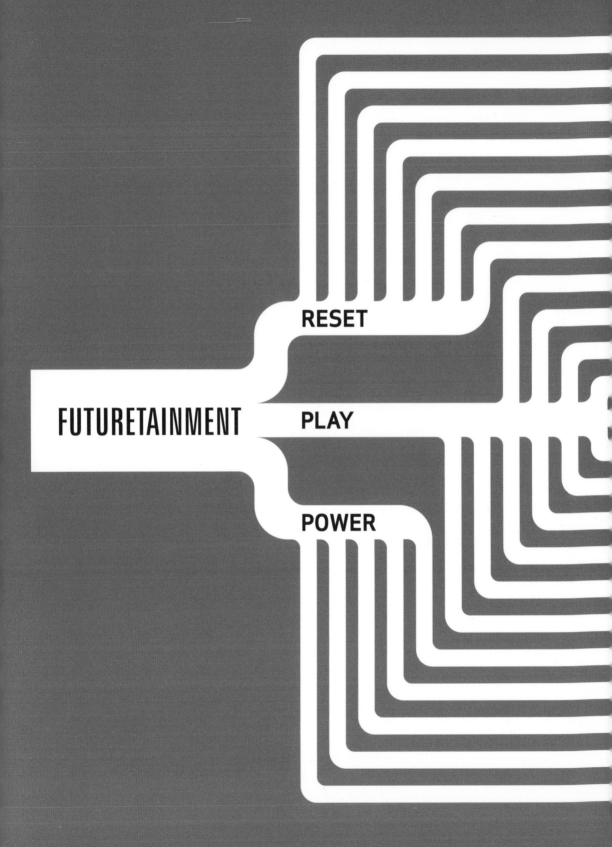

FUTURETAINMENT

RESET

PLAY

POWER

1. REVOLUTION   10

2. FACTORY   34

3. MEDIAJACK   42

4. NETWORK   54

5. UBIQUITY   64

6. WHERE   80

7. CROWD   92

8. SOCIAL   104

9. DISCOVERY   116

10. VIRAL   126

11. AVATAR   140

12. LIFECAST   152

13. PULSE   164

14. AUTHENTIC   170

15. TAG   176

16. SHIFT   184

17. MASH   194

18. IMMERSE   204

19. META   214

20. SLICE   220

21. PLATFORM   234

22. ENGAGE   244

23. DISRUPT   256

YESTERDAY THE W

◀ R

NOW IT'S YOUR T

WORLD CHANGED

RESET

URN

PART 1

1. REVOLUTION

CHANGE ALW

APPEARS IN

UNTIL IT'S T

WAYS

CREMENTAL

OO

LATE

Welcome to the Revolution.

Please don't be too alarmed if you haven't noticed; we have grown so accustomed to technology constantly improving around us that sometimes it is difficult to make the distinction between what is new and what is different. Like sitting too close to a TV screen, on which thousands of small changes are taking place all at once, it is impossible to see what it all means until you step back and take a look at the picture as a whole.

Consider this: millions of total strangers are linked by online social networks; more videos are being downloaded every moment than used to be broadcast over an entire year, only a few years ago; enormous server farms of user-generated content are constantly being created; ever-more powerful personal devices and an expanding web of wireless broadband ensure that wherever we are, so is the network.

We are accelerating towards a time when every piece of content ever made will be instantly available to anyone, anywhere.

It might be tempting to see this as nothing more than the inexorable progress of technology, but there is more to it than that. The changes that we are witnessing have very little to do with faster hardware or smarter software – they are all about people.

A television is a glowing image inside a box.

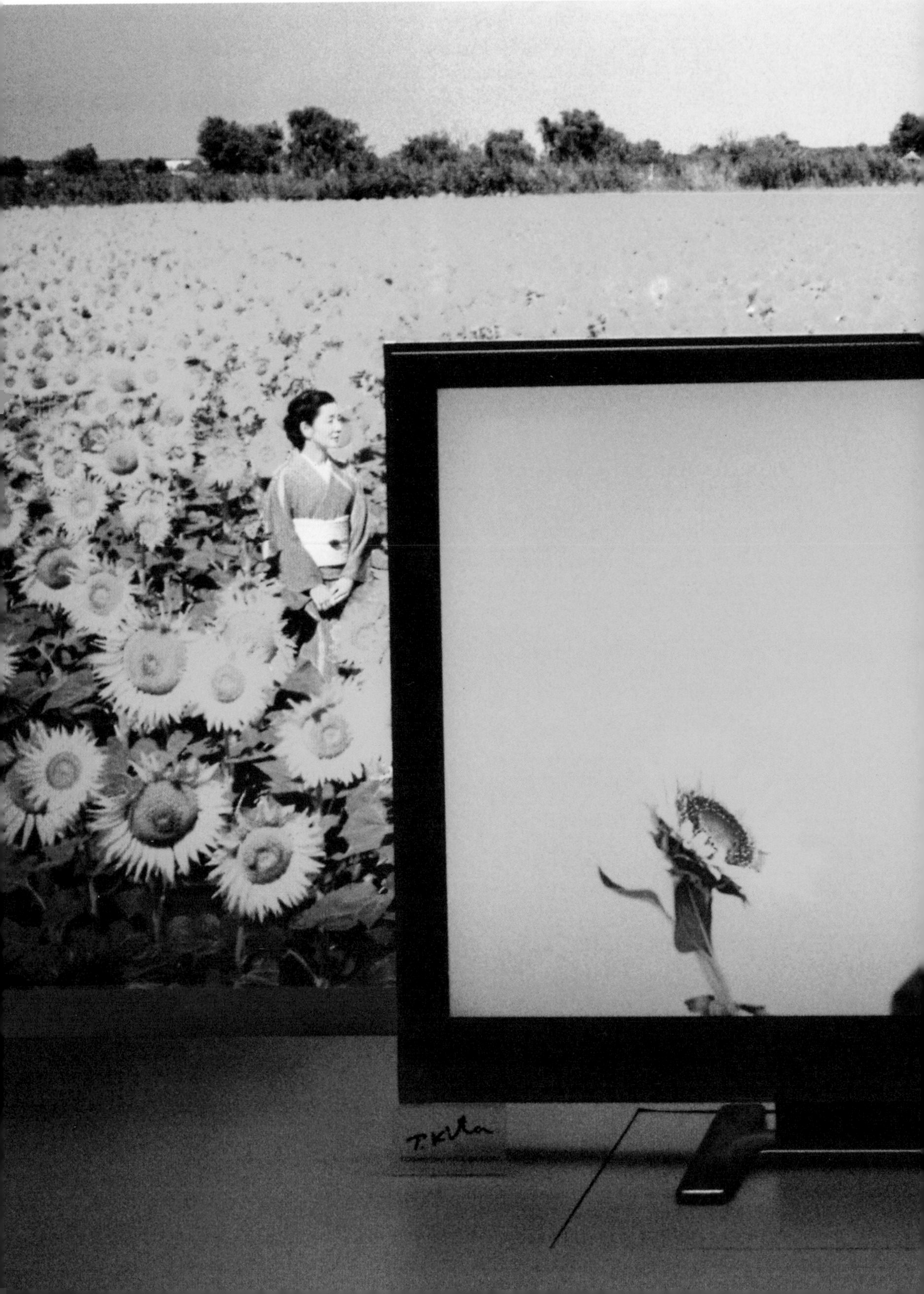

A cinema is a big moving picture in a darkened room.

For the most part, however, media is not really about the physical or technological side of things, it is more about behaviour.

The technology of television may have changed over the last fifty years – from black and white to colour, from analogue to digital, from standard definition to high definition – but watching television as a behaviour (sitting at home, changing channels) remained largely the same.

But what happens when the consumers start acting differently? What happens when they stop sitting on a couch with a remote control and begin searching for video clips, building their own playlists of entertainment, pausing live television, forwarding TV shows to other people, discussing what to watch online and viewing content when and where it suits them? Is that still television? I don't think so.

You might expect evolution in media to be driven purely by improvements in quality, such as better reception, better imagery or better sound, but in fact the opposite is true. People have embraced low-fidelity MP3 audio over CD formats, and web videos over high-definition DVDs for the simple reason that digital media has opened up new possibilities for consumption that simply didn't exist before.

The way in which consumers are behaving today indicates the birth of something entirely different – an interactive digital world.

There is a new generation that understands digital media without explanation. For them, interactive technology is not something they need to learn – it is entirely natural.

In 1994, Netscape released its first web browser. Suddenly, information from all over the world could be accessed via a series of mouse clicks. To the new generation born after this momentous event, the world of libraries, record stores and postal deliveries in which many of us had grown up seemed entirely alien.

By the time the children of this new generation were ten years old, most of the world's music was available almost instantaneously, either for free or at a very low cost. When they reached their fifteenth birthdays, the same applied to movies and TV shows and, by the time they arrive at the age of twenty, there will probably be little remaining that is not available at the click of a button.

Who are these people? They are not revolutionaries; they are the children of the revolution. They are not trying to change the world; they have simply never known any other. I like to think of them as Naturals.

In terms of entertainment products, what seems natural to them is unnatural to us. They are unfamiliar with our traditional concepts such as region coding, programme schedules, copyright protection, selective distribution, release windows and purchasing entire albums rather than selected tracks.

The world that this generation of Naturals will go on to create, both for themselves and for us, can be anticipated by watching the behaviour of teenagers all over the world, and especially in countries such as China, where an entirely new media ecosystem has emerged.

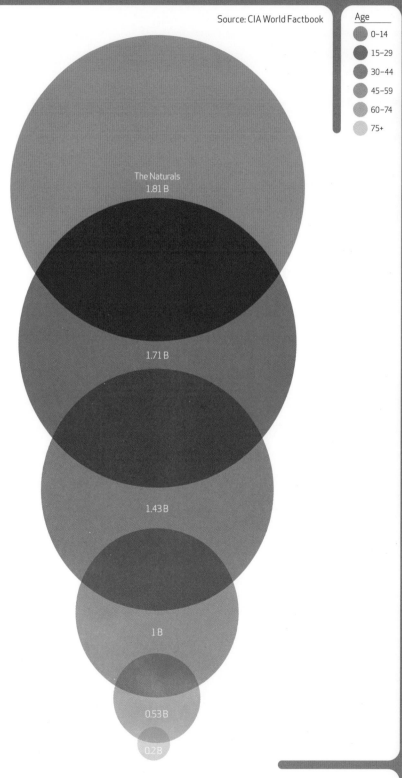

Source: CIA World Factbook

Age
- 0–14
- 15–29
- 30–44
- 45–59
- 60–74
- 75+

The Naturals
1.81 B

1.71 B

1.43 B

1 B

0.53 B

0.2 B

Nearly a third of the population of the world is currently under the age of fifteen.
This group form the demographic cohort known as 'The Naturals'

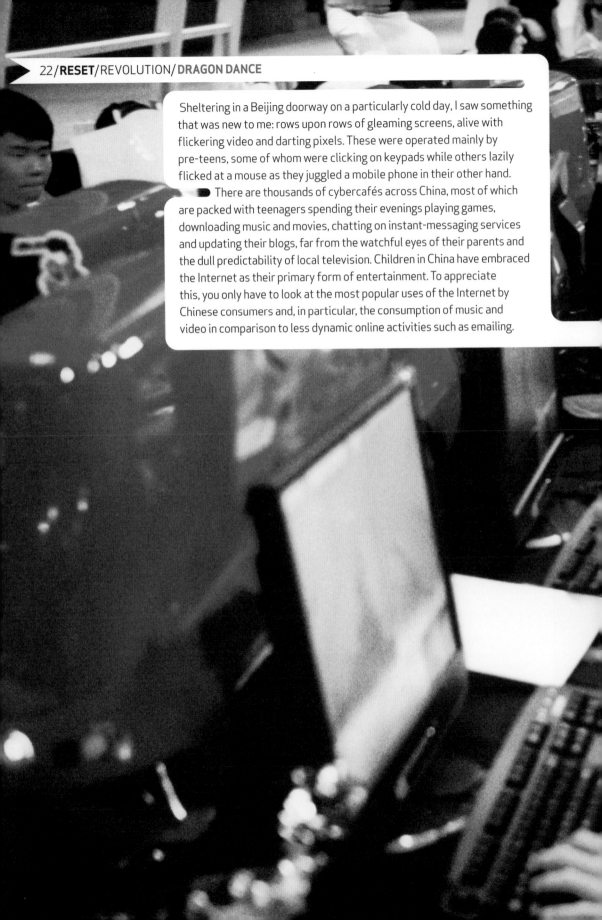

Sheltering in a Beijing doorway on a particularly cold day, I saw something that was new to me: rows upon rows of gleaming screens, alive with flickering video and darting pixels. These were operated mainly by pre-teens, some of whom were clicking on keypads while others lazily flicked at a mouse as they juggled a mobile phone in their other hand.

There are thousands of cybercafés across China, most of which are packed with teenagers spending their evenings playing games, downloading music and movies, chatting on instant-messaging services and updating their blogs, far from the watchful eyes of their parents and the dull predictability of local television. Children in China have embraced the Internet as their primary form of entertainment. To appreciate this, you only have to look at the most popular uses of the Internet by Chinese consumers and, in particular, the consumption of music and video in comparison to less dynamic online activities such as emailing.

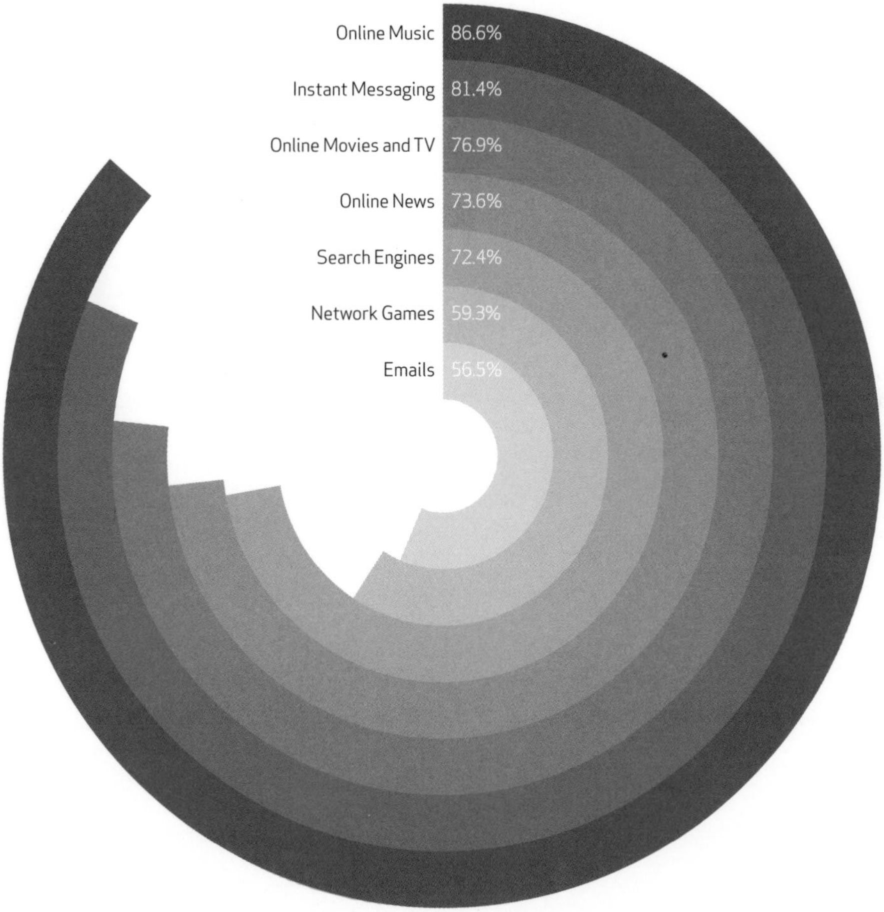

Online Music 86.6%
Instant Messaging 81.4%
Online Movies and TV 76.9%
Online News 73.6%
Search Engines 72.4%
Network Games 59.3%
Emails 56.5%

What Chinese Users Do Online – Source: CNNIC JAN 2008

More than 200 million people in China chat regularly on social networks such as QQ, while multiplayer fantasy games can pit players from small villages against those from big cities. Despite restrictions on conventional TV broadcasting, Chinese youngsters have the world's TV and movie libraries at their fingertips – uploaded and even translated on local video-sharing networks. In fact, illegal file-trading is so rampant that music labels have given up on trying to make any significant profit from conventional CD sales, instead focusing increasingly on live events, endorsements, merchandise and ringtones.

This phenomenon is not just limited to China. There is a new generation of young urban consumers around the world that has grown up with more freedom and global awareness than any before. From Hollywood movies to Korean pop culture, Japanese manga and Hong Kong celebrities – young audiences are exposed to an ever-expanding range of entertainment and lifestyle choices. Quite at home with instant messaging, peer-to-peer television, virtual worlds, blogs and multiplayer gaming, they have never known a world in which fun was not available on demand. They are enthusiastically involved, too, discussing the latest issues, entertainment and consumer brands on blogs and bulletin-board sites. There are more than 80 million blogs in China alone.

The entertainment celebrities in this generation's world are not only famous actors and models, but also everyday people who have achieved 'Netstar' status through the popularity of their blogs or viral videos. Nouveau web celebrities such as the Backdorm Boys, Furong JieJie, Tian Xian Mei Mei and Xiao Pang have used their online popularity to further their careers, resulting in movie deals and commercial sponsorships for soft drinks, mobile phones and sports clothing.

If you are a savvy teenager, all this entertainment is available very simply. The latest music can be easily found and downloaded from the front pages of major search engines, while video-sharing sites host an array of content from across the world.

However, although a huge amount of content can be downloaded for free, this certainly doesn't mean that there is no business in online entertainment. Whether connected to a game or a social network, some of the most popular and profitable business models are based entirely on selling digital merchandise such as ringtones, virtual items, personalized avatars and artificial currencies that are powerful enough to give central banks cause for concern. That is why companies such as Tencent, which operates the QQ brand in China, are able to make close to US$500 million in profit, with only a fraction of that amount coming from traditional online advertising.

It's entertainment, but not as you know it.

If you take a walk through the area around St Paul's Cathedral in London, you will find the Stationers' Hall, one of the few ancient Livery Halls remaining in the City of London.

The trade guild known as 'The Worshipful Company of Stationers and Newspaper Makers' has existed for more than 600 years. It originally held a monopoly over the publishing industry and was officially responsible for setting and enforcing copyright regulations. However, despite its long history of power and influence, in the spring of 2006 the downfall of the traditional newspaper was predicted by one of the greatest media moguls of all, Rupert Murdoch.

'Power is moving away from the old elite in our industry – the editors, the chief executives and, let's face it, the proprietors,' he warned the assembled crowd. 'A new generation of media consumers has arisen, demanding content delivered when they want it, how they want it, and very much as they want it.'

This was true, but a question remained: what could be done about it? Up until now, the power of the media had always been directly related to the amount of control that a company had – circulation deals, exclusive broadcasting rights, even a motley crew of newspaper stands and delivery boys. Media companies were attempting not only to create great content but also, more importantly, to control and enlarge its distribution. Therefore, companies were continually striving to acquire additional links in the media chain; the more links they owned (distribution business, TV station, newspapers, etc.), the more control they had, and therefore the more money they could make.

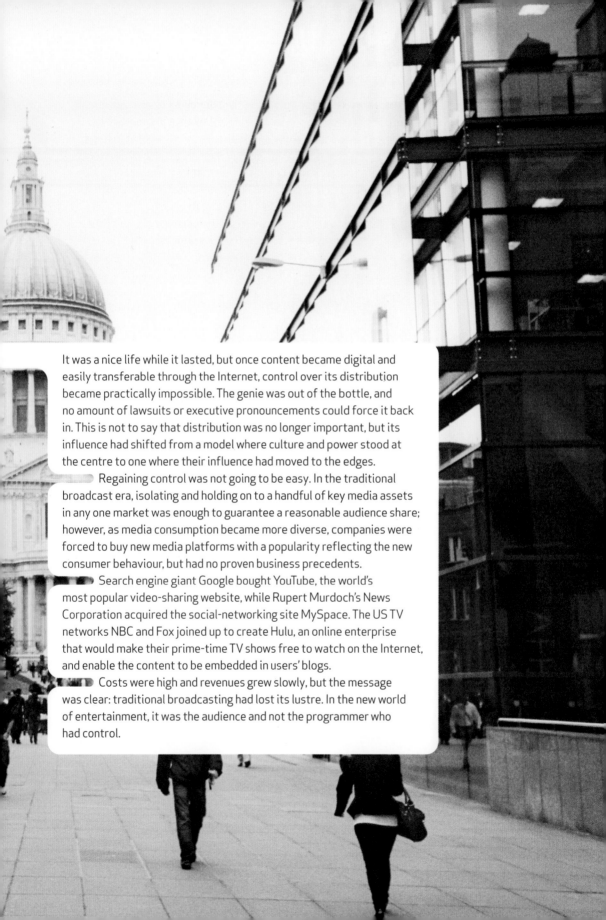

It was a nice life while it lasted, but once content became digital and easily transferable through the Internet, control over its distribution became practically impossible. The genie was out of the bottle, and no amount of lawsuits or executive pronouncements could force it back in. This is not to say that distribution was no longer important, but its influence had shifted from a model where culture and power stood at the centre to one where their influence had moved to the edges.

Regaining control was not going to be easy. In the traditional broadcast era, isolating and holding on to a handful of key media assets in any one market was enough to guarantee a reasonable audience share; however, as media consumption became more diverse, companies were forced to buy new media platforms with a popularity reflecting the new consumer behaviour, but had no proven business precedents.

Search engine giant Google bought YouTube, the world's most popular video-sharing website, while Rupert Murdoch's News Corporation acquired the social-networking site MySpace. The US TV networks NBC and Fox joined up to create Hulu, an online enterprise that would make their prime-time TV shows free to watch on the Internet, and enable the content to be embedded in users' blogs.

Costs were high and revenues grew slowly, but the message was clear: traditional broadcasting had lost its lustre. In the new world of entertainment, it was the audience and not the programmer who had control.

Networks are a key concept in media. Whether describing a distribution, advertising or content network, the original concept of a media network is based on the simple premise of broadcasting: one person talking to many. In a traditional broadcast network, there is a central tower sending out a signal to everyone in a nearby area. It is an efficient and effective means of distribution, assuming that everyone is happy to watch the same thing at the same time.

However, in a world where every piece of content is available to anyone at anytime, there is no need for broadcast towers to beam everything out. Consumers can watch anything they want, so how do they choose? Quite simply, people start to rely on a different kind of network: an Audience Network.

Audience Networks are human-based; rather than relying on satellites or transmitter towers, consumers access content via links with other consumers. Those links might be direct (a referral from a friend), or indirect (generated from a large list of recommendations). The crucial difference from how a traditional media network works, is that the interaction of people within the new network makes it smarter.

You can find Audience Networks everywhere: a circle of friends connected via an instant-messaging program, a group of business associates joined on a business-networking site such as Linkedin, teenagers blogging about their favourite online personality, a celebrity with a million followers on Twitter, a network of electro fans on Facebook, or a statistically similar set of book-buyers on Amazon.

Audience Networks and their interactions are not necessarily planned or centrally organized.

A major consequence of these networks is that, in the future, everyone who interacts with a piece of content will subtly change the experience for other consumers. It could be as simple as just watching something and sharing a comment about it with friends online, or as complex as using web-based tools to classify, remix, recommend, personalize or redistribute content.

Audiences may act locally, but the result of their behaviour will be global.

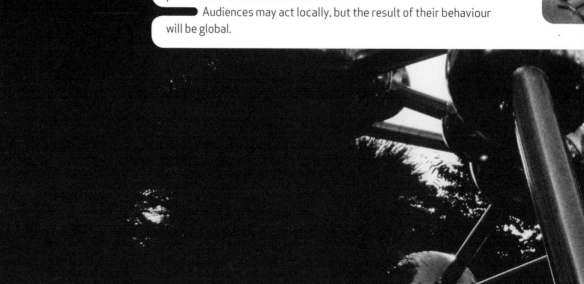

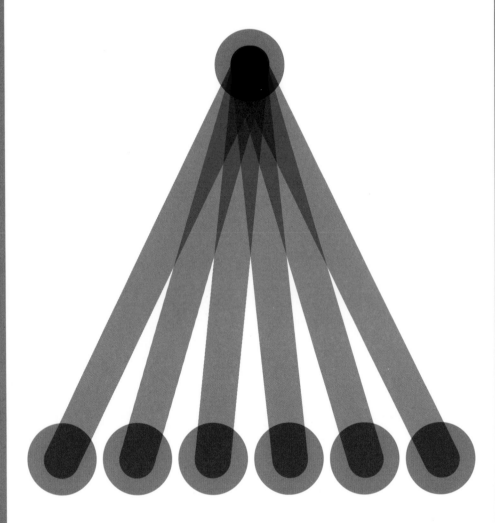

Broadcast Network

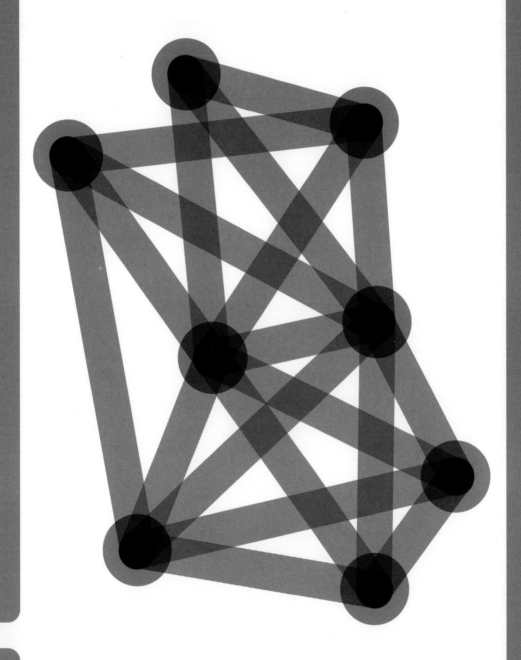

Audience Network

How did all this change so suddenly?

It is to do with momentum. New patterns of behaviour often build to a point of criticality that is then followed by a rapid state change. This is called the Cliff Effect, and it is the reason why the digital media revolution may well play out faster than many will expect.

The problem with predicting such change is that consumer behaviour can sometimes appear illogical. The sound quality of MP3s is far inferior to that of CDs, camera phones take much lower resolution images than film cameras, and web-streamed videos offer poorer picture quality than DVDs. Yet all of these mediums have thrived at the expense of their higher resolution alternatives. Clearly, to consumers utility is a more powerful incentive than fidelity.

Despite what company executives might like to think, revolutions in media are rarely based on linear improvements in technology – they are ignited when people start to behave differently. Radical change is a break away from previous forms of behaviour. At first, it can sometimes look like a step backwards, but it is simply a step in a different direction.

So where will this lead us? To find the answer, first of all we need to look at where we have been.

INSIGHT 1. REVOLUTION

There is a revolution taking place, and it has little to do with technology. People are changing the way they discover, share and consume media – and that will turn every aspect of the traditional content business upside down. The new generation understands this intuitively. They have grown up surrounded by the Web, and have never known a world where entertainment is not instantly available; anywhere, anytime and on any device. For them, digital media is not something new, it is entirely natural.

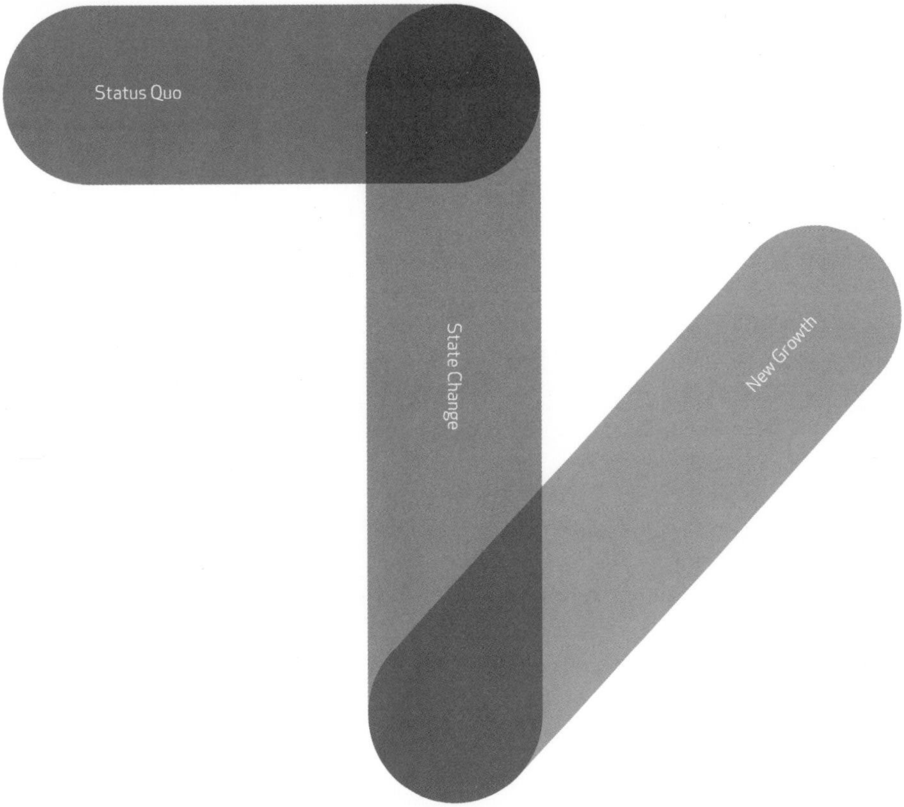

Status Quo

State Change

New Growth

The Cliff Effect

MASS PR

MEDIA M

MAKE WA

MEDIA PR

BY THE M

ODUCED

UST

Y FOR 2. FACTORY

ODUCED

ASSES

If you ever have the chance to visit a newspaper printing plant, seize the opportunity, quickly, before it's too late. You will see something amazing, something vast, loud and impossibly mechanical: a room the size of a football field filled with machinery, hundreds of human operators, newsprint rolls the size of small trucks and long chains of automated grippers rushing overhead, all steeped in the slightly acidic smell of ink. You can watch media being assembled right before your eyes, like the products of a magical Willy Wonka chocolate factory.

And until recently, of course, the media was just that: a product-based industry. It related to something that was made, sold and consumed; something produced by an agglomeration of workers in the Factory. Here, everyone's job in the production process was clear: the people in charge decided what was made. Studio bigwigs cut deals over lunch, music-label executives bartered fame with starlets and newspaper editors decided what was newsworthy.

Once they were finished, an army of thousands of journalists, TV producers, movie directors, artists, sound engineers and production assistants made the projects happen. Like the credits of a Hollywood blockbuster, the scale of production required for glossy pieces of entertainment seemed to grow with each successive year.

When everything was ready, media companies would use their carefully controlled relationships to distribute their product. Master tapes were couriered to TV stations and film prints dispatched to cinema chains, while trucks, paperboys and supply chains transported neatly shrink-wrapped CDs, DVDs and print products to shops and street corners.

Finally, the marketing people had the unenviable job of convincing the public that they needed to buy what the people in charge wanted them to have. At the end of the process, the consumers largely took what they were given. It was a perfect example of top-down control.

Perhaps not everyone liked what the Factory made all the time. Sometimes there were no interesting stories in the newspapers, or there was nothing on television, but consumers mostly continued to read and watch regardless. With new channels, magazines and other products arriving almost every day, it felt as if they had control over their media – almost.

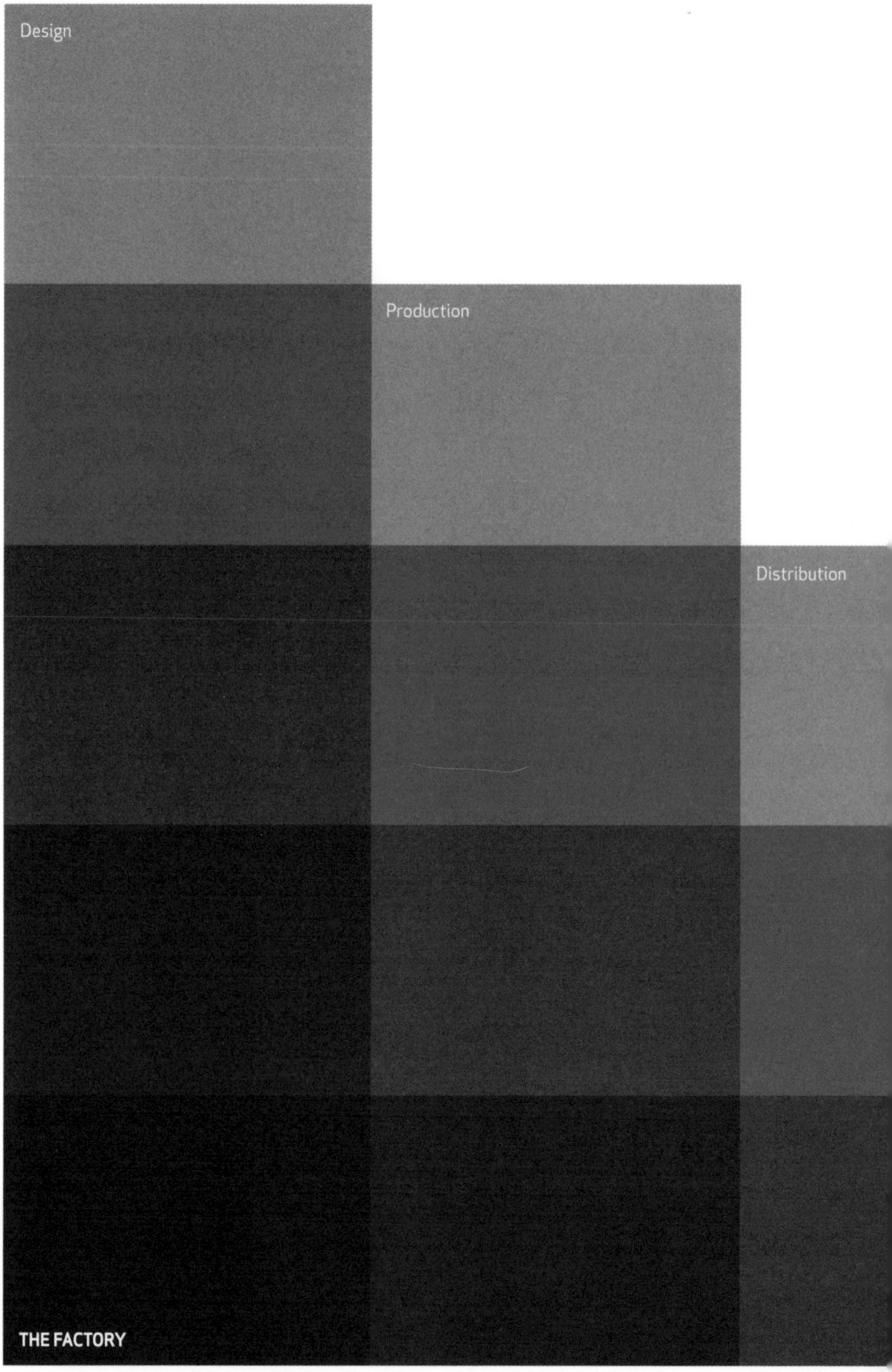

Design

Production

Distribution

THE FACTORY

In the Factory, media was a shrink-wrapped product designed for mass consumption. That is, until consumers stopped behaving themselves.

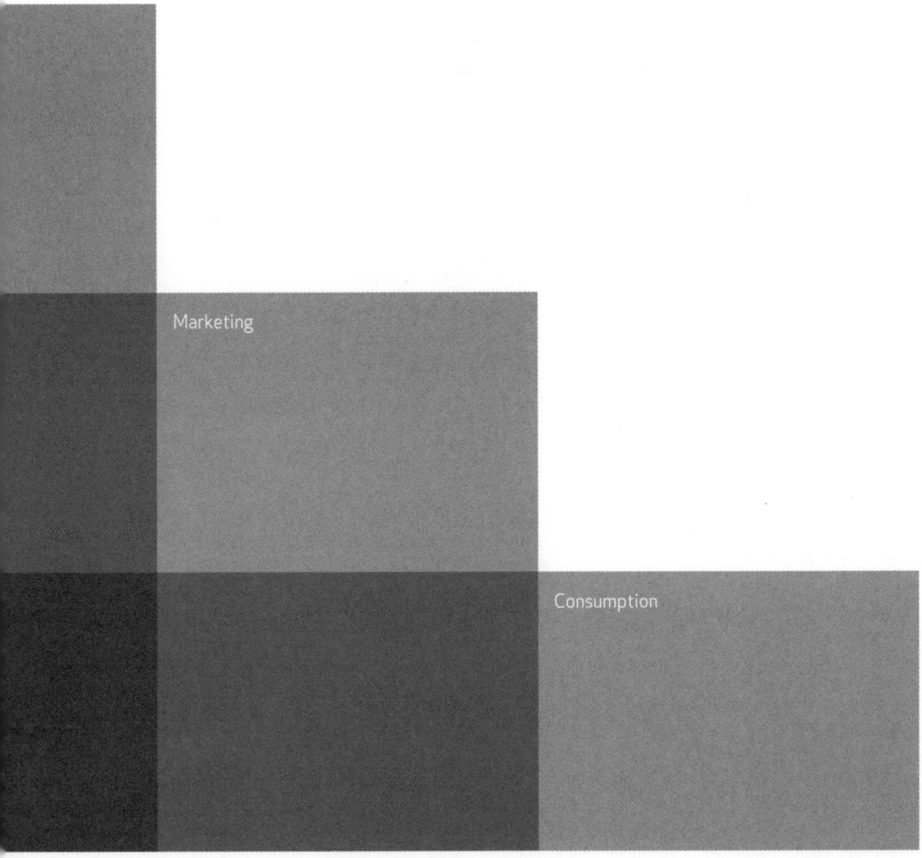

Marketing

Consumption

At some point, the Factory exploded – although not everyone will admit to it, even now.

The great thing about the Factory was its predictability. The world's most successful investor, Warren Buffet, used to love the newspaper industry because with good management, in a town with a growing population, it was certain that circulation and profits would increase with time.

Even better was the Factory's chain-like production process. You made a big-budget movie, for instance, and spent a fortune promoting its opening weekend. With the resulting publicity you could sell the movie to TV and cable networks worldwide, before unleashing countless DVDs, music spin-offs and other merchandising. When the feature was no longer making enough money, you filmed the sequel.

But, all of a sudden, things started to look a little uncertain for the Factory model:

CD sales dropped drastically.

TV viewing figures started to fall.

DVD sales hit a plateau in the West, and fell off the cliff altogether in many Asian countries.

Radio stations played less music.

Piracy increased.

It became more difficult to limit distribution to a particular region or timescale.

Box office openings attracted less interest (and therefore made less money).

However, this didn't mean that entertainment had become less popular. On the contrary, given the amount of discussion, sharing, blogging and online interaction going on, entertainment seemed to be enjoying a veritable renaissance. There was just one major change: entertainment content was not necessarily being consumed in the form that had been approved by the Factory for distribution. Audiences were hijacking the media.

INSIGHT 2. FACTORY

Think of the production of traditional media in the shape of a Factory. Content was made by professionals, marketed by experts and distributed through authorized channels. Everyone was happy with the arrangement, until the Web arrived. Suddenly, audiences were no longer content to simply watch, listen and read what they were given. Consumers had taken control from media moguls.

YOU CAN'T STOP THE MUSIC

3. MEDIAJACK

Revered in Japan for his endless pursuit of innovation and creativity, Dr Yoshiro Nakamatsu is not your average scientist. He holds hundreds of patents for his inventions, eats a strict diet to maintain peak brain functions, and has photographed and retrospectively analysed every meal he has consumed for the last thirty years.

To keep himself inspired, Dr Nakamatsu created three specially designed spaces. The first room was 'static', with white walls, a rock garden and a five-ton boulder from Kyoto. The second was 'dynamic', with black-and-white-striped walls, leather furniture and special audio and video equipment. The third was not a room at all – it was underwater.

It was while holding his breath at the bottom of his swimming pool that Dr Nakamatsu came up with the idea of the compact disc.

When music first started being released on CD, audiophiles rejected the digital sound as being acoustically inferior to their high-end analogue systems. They may have had a point, but for consumers who were listening to music on low-fidelity cassette tapes, digitally sampled music on CD was a dramatic improvement. Another advantage was that, unlike tapes, CDs didn't wear out.

More importantly, however, for the massive changes that would soon occur in the entertainment industry, the conversion of analogue content into binary information (in this case represented by laser-etched pits on a disc) was the critical first step to an even bigger idea: no physical medium at all and the beginning of a new digital era in the music industry.

Media products were traditionally designed to be consumed in fixed physical formats, in defined markets and at specific times. Of course, formats were also incredibly limiting and often, for the content stored on them, fatal. Music recorded on forgotten formats, 8-track cartridges for example, has been doomed to silence.

But thanks to the CD, and later the DVD, media products became digital. Once people worked out how to liberate the content from the discs, it became easily portable. As a result of the potential of the Internet, content became searchable and easy to exchange and reproduce. Audiences had previously been forced to consume entertainment in the manner that the media bosses dictated, but once digitization and web distribution had freed content from its constraining modes of production, consumers began to question the old way of doing things.

Why buy an entire album, when you could download the one song you wanted?

Why wait months for the latest hit movie or TV show to air in your country, when you could get the same content from the Web?

With content from all over the world only a click away, why limit your viewing to the listings in your local TV guide?

Why believe mainstream marketers who tell you what is worthy of your attention when your friends are a far more reliable source of information?

Now detached from its original media formats, content became more malleable; it could be moulded and changed more easily – in other words, it had become hackable.

The concept of hacking is a throwback to the early days of computers and coding; when something is hackable, it can be modified by its users. Entertainment products, no longer hermetically sealed, could be broken down, remixed, stored in different formats and transferred around. For a media company that relies on a specific format as a tool of control and profit, this can be disastrous.

Over the last fifty years, we have seen a wide range of formats come and go: vinyl records, 8-track cartridges, cassette tapes, VHS, Betamax, DAT tapes, Mini DV tapes, MiniDiscs, Laser Discs, CDs, DVDs, UMD discs, memory sticks, HD-DVDs – the list goes on. From the average consumer's point of view, this often meant that an investment in a particular mode of technology was suddenly rendered useless, as the format became obsolete.

The concept of a media format is now a relic from the time in which the medium was more powerful than the message; when determining the container was equivalent to controlling the content.

For almost as long as the Internet has been around, consumers have been using it to share digital entertainment content, transposed into compressed formats for easy distribution. They were not only sharing pop music, but also vintage TV shows, the latest movies, rare vinyl records – even antiquarian books and retro magazines. They worked out how to transfer their CD collections to their computers, digitize TV shows and exchange them via BitTorrent, crack the encryption code of DVDs and watch movies on their iPods.

Suburbia had discovered Mediajacking.

Mediajacking involves using digital sampling technology to liberate content from the restrictions of its original medium, or Digital Rights Management restrictions, so that it can be distributed, modified and consumed on any digital-capable device. Mediajacking is illegal, but it is surprising how the inconvenience of obtaining content legally can turn people towards it. Media companies have had to realize that if they don't make their content readily available, consumers will make it available for them through illegal channels. Mediajacking presents a major problem for content and copyright owners worldwide, but it points to a critical insight: consumers value convenience over quality. In the absence of an easy legal alternative, a large percentage of the population will make do with a low-resolution copy of a favourite TV show or movie in preference to waiting for the high-quality, high-definition DVD version to appear in their local store.

Anne Sweeney, then president of the Disney-ABC television group, once described how a celebration of the ratings success for 'Desperate Housewives' was ruined when an employee showed her a copy of an episode obtained via BitTorrent just fifteen minutes after the programme was broadcast. It was not long afterwards that the company cut their first deal with iTunes for web distribution.

If Mediajacking demonstrates the ability of consumers to circumvent the system, it also raises a more difficult question: what is the real value of entertainment content if people can easily obtain it for nothing?

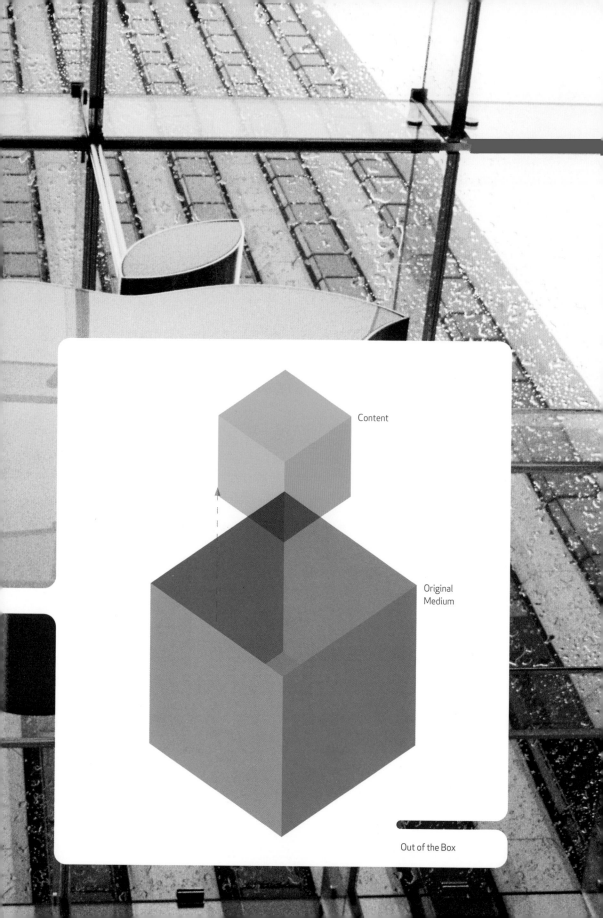

Content

Original
Medium

Out of the Box

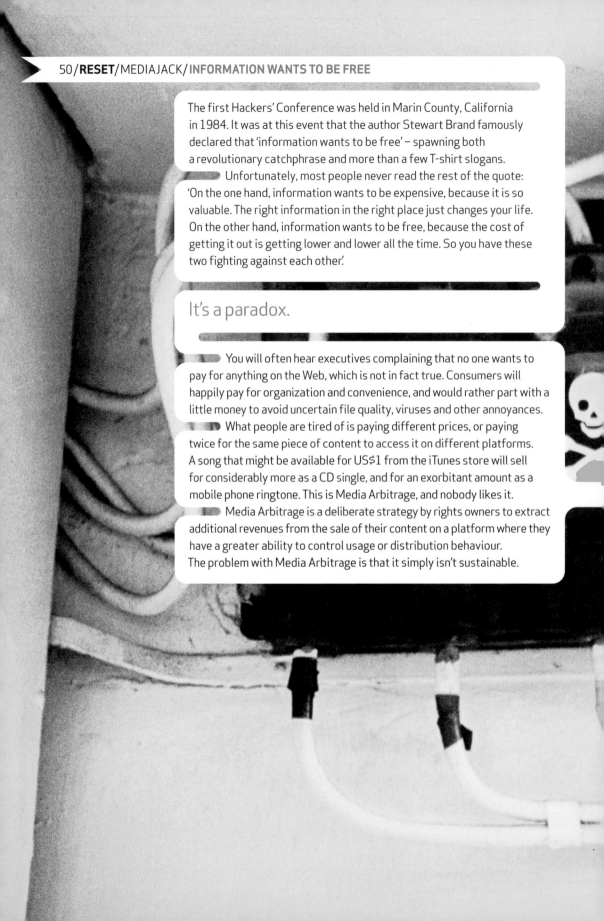

The first Hackers' Conference was held in Marin County, California in 1984. It was at this event that the author Stewart Brand famously declared that 'information wants to be free' – spawning both a revolutionary catchphrase and more than a few T-shirt slogans.

Unfortunately, most people never read the rest of the quote: 'On the one hand, information wants to be expensive, because it is so valuable. The right information in the right place just changes your life. On the other hand, information wants to be free, because the cost of getting it out is getting lower and lower all the time. So you have these two fighting against each other'.

It's a paradox.

You will often hear executives complaining that no one wants to pay for anything on the Web, which is not in fact true. Consumers will happily pay for organization and convenience, and would rather part with a little money to avoid uncertain file quality, viruses and other annoyances.

What people are tired of is paying different prices, or paying twice for the same piece of content to access it on different platforms. A song that might be available for US$1 from the iTunes store will sell for considerably more as a CD single, and for an exorbitant amount as a mobile phone ringtone. This is Media Arbitrage, and nobody likes it.

Media Arbitrage is a deliberate strategy by rights owners to extract additional revenues from the sale of their content on a platform where they have a greater ability to control usage or distribution behaviour. The problem with Media Arbitrage is that it simply isn't sustainable.

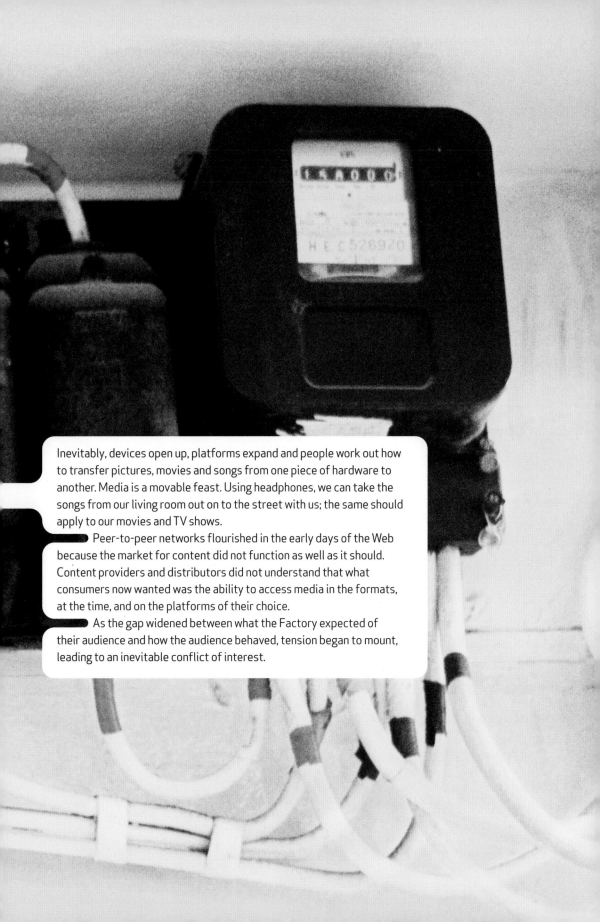

Inevitably, devices open up, platforms expand and people work out how to transfer pictures, movies and songs from one piece of hardware to another. Media is a movable feast. Using headphones, we can take the songs from our living room out on to the street with us; the same should apply to our movies and TV shows.

   Peer-to-peer networks flourished in the early days of the Web because the market for content did not function as well as it should. Content providers and distributors did not understand that what consumers now wanted was the ability to access media in the formats, at the time, and on the platforms of their choice.

   As the gap widened between what the Factory expected of their audience and how the audience behaved, tension began to mount, leading to an inevitable conflict of interest.

Many of my clients have asked me over the years how they can spot innovation in their industry; I always reply that the best place to look is in the legal department. The next big idea is probably sitting on the top of a pile of documents relating to people you are about to sue. Copyright infringement letters, injunctions, take-down notices – the legal system is the first friction point between existing traditions and the cutting edge.

The headlines are full of it: Napster vs. Big Music, BitTorrent v. Hollywood, bloggers vs. brand owners. Some of the defendants are criminals, but many are just ordinary people who, like millions of others, are seeking new ways in which to consume entertainment.

Evolution is never as seamless as we would like to believe. Media dinosaurs still roam the earth: even in decline, newspapers continue to make huge profits, people still buy CDs and TV networks still sell plenty of advertising on the strength of their linear broadcasting – for now, at least.

But if you look closely enough, you will see a new pattern unfolding.

INSIGHT 3. MEDIAJACK

There is no point in trying to fight the future. Formats, rights, and playback limitations aside, consumers will always find a way to get to the content they want, even if that means transferring content across media platorms. Yet Mediajacking is not about breaking the rules. It is just a symptom of a media regime yet to adjust to changes in consumer behaviour.

CONNECTED

NE IS

4. NETWORK

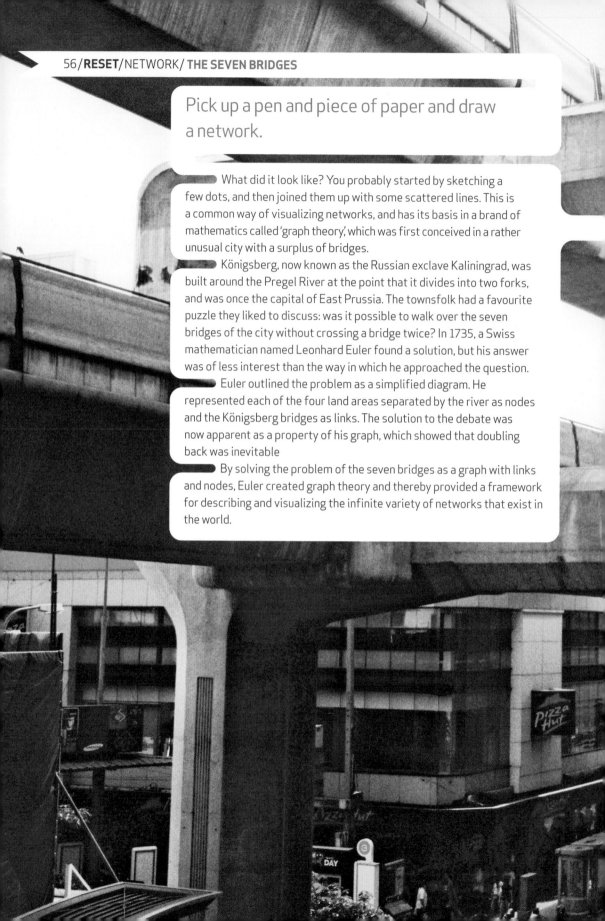

Pick up a pen and piece of paper and draw a network.

What did it look like? You probably started by sketching a few dots, and then joined them up with some scattered lines. This is a common way of visualizing networks, and has its basis in a brand of mathematics called 'graph theory', which was first conceived in a rather unusual city with a surplus of bridges.

Königsberg, now known as the Russian exclave Kaliningrad, was built around the Pregel River at the point that it divides into two forks, and was once the capital of East Prussia. The townsfolk had a favourite puzzle they liked to discuss: was it possible to walk over the seven bridges of the city without crossing a bridge twice? In 1735, a Swiss mathematician named Leonhard Euler found a solution, but his answer was of less interest than the way in which he approached the question.

Euler outlined the problem as a simplified diagram. He represented each of the four land areas separated by the river as nodes and the Königsberg bridges as links. The solution to the debate was now apparent as a property of his graph, which showed that doubling back was inevitable

By solving the problem of the seven bridges as a graph with links and nodes, Euler created graph theory and thereby provided a framework for describing and visualizing the infinite variety of networks that exist in the world.

Seven Bridges of Königsberg

Consider for a moment Euler's diagram, replacing the nodes of land with people and the bridges with the media which they consume. What kind of network would that be? How would it grow? What rules would govern its dynamics and interactions?

It's what you might call an Audience Network.

An Audience Network describes the relationships that consumers of entertainment products have with content and with each other. Unlike the bridges of Königsberg, the links of an Audience Network are not fixed, but are constantly growing, shifting and rewiring themselves. In the era of the Factory, the audience for a particular TV show was defined by its broadcast schedule – for example, the million or so people who had their televisions switched on at 8 p.m. on a Tuesday evening. However, the concept of an 'audience' is already changing, and in future it is likely that it will be very different.

Let us imagine a scenario: Wendy hears about a new comedy show called 'The Apartment' from her friend Jack. She loves the show and decides to post a short review of it on her blog, embedding a scene on her profile page. Sue and Liu are friends of Wendy, and discover the show from her post. Lucy doesn't know Wendy personally but she reads her blog every now and then; she reposts the clip from Wendy's site, with some of her own thoughts, and her friends Ben and Rick find out about the show. Ben adds the show to his personal playlist, along with a rating. As other people do the same, the show's popularity increases. Fred and Chu keep an eye on popular shows on their media aggregation service and notice the growing number of positive ratings for the comedy, so they download an episode and so it continues.

It is a pattern that will gradually become more commonplace. As more and more people interact with entertainment content and each other, their actions create links that multiply the paths to the original content. It may not be instantaneous, but if 'The Apartment' appeals to enough people, over time it will attract an audience. Unlike a traditional broadcast network that feeds content from one to many, content in an Audience Network spreads entertainment content from many to many.

Everyone in an Audience Network is connected to everyone else.

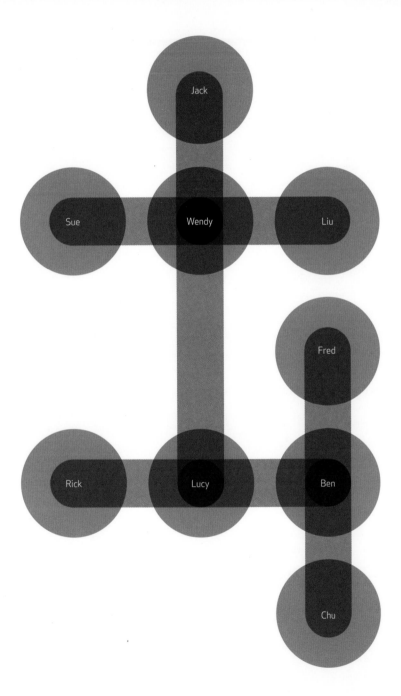

Audience Network

I once visited the headquarters of Google in Mountain View, California. It's an odd place that could be described as a blend of one part university campus and one part day spa, with a dash of seventies cosmic cult aesthetics thrown in for good measure. The clock had just turned on the new millennium and the company was rapidly expanding. Anyone who had been in a relatively senior position at Google for a few years had probably made enough money to retire already.

A friend of mine who was retiring from the company later that week took me on a backstage tour of the building. Along the way, he showed me the company's first server. Unlike the usual tangle of wires in an office network, this one was neatly arranged along a central spine.

'Nice,' I said, looking the artefact up and down. 'Was your first network engineer a neat freak?'

'Actually, the guy who set it up used to be a neurosurgeon,' my friend said with a wry smile. 'We think he was trying to make it look like the spinal cord.'

I couldn't work out whether or not he was joking, but given the density of highly educated people in the building, it seemed strange enough to be true. In any case, it was certainly an appropriate metaphor, because in many ways Google worked in a similar way to a brain.

Google's founders were inspired by the way in which academics use citations to lend authority to their research papers, and decided to use similar means to deduce which web pages were more important than others. The idea was simple: the more links that existed to a piece of content from other places, the more relevant it must be to the topic in hand. It was one of the first attempts to make use of the natural order created when Audience Networks described and categorized the content they consumed.

The technique worked fabulously. If you typed BMW or Jaguar into the search engine, you would usually get the car manufacturer's home page, because no matter how diverse the millions of pages on the Web that talked about cars might have been, they would generally all link to the official corporate page. Of course, the flipside was also true: if no one linked to you at all, you might as well not have existed.

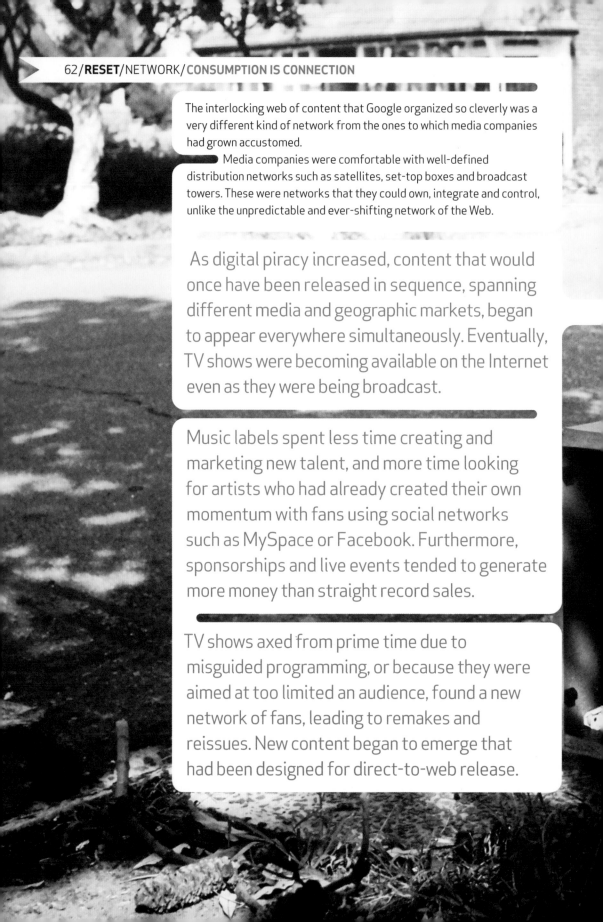

The interlocking web of content that Google organized so cleverly was a very different kind of network from the ones to which media companies had grown accustomed.

Media companies were comfortable with well-defined distribution networks such as satellites, set-top boxes and broadcast towers. These were networks that they could own, integrate and control, unlike the unpredictable and ever-shifting network of the Web.

As digital piracy increased, content that would once have been released in sequence, spanning different media and geographic markets, began to appear everywhere simultaneously. Eventually, TV shows were becoming available on the Internet even as they were being broadcast.

Music labels spent less time creating and marketing new talent, and more time looking for artists who had already created their own momentum with fans using social networks such as MySpace or Facebook. Furthermore, sponsorships and live events tended to generate more money than straight record sales.

TV shows axed from prime time due to misguided programming, or because they were aimed at too limited an audience, found a new network of fans, leading to remakes and reissues. New content began to emerge that had been designed for direct-to-web release.

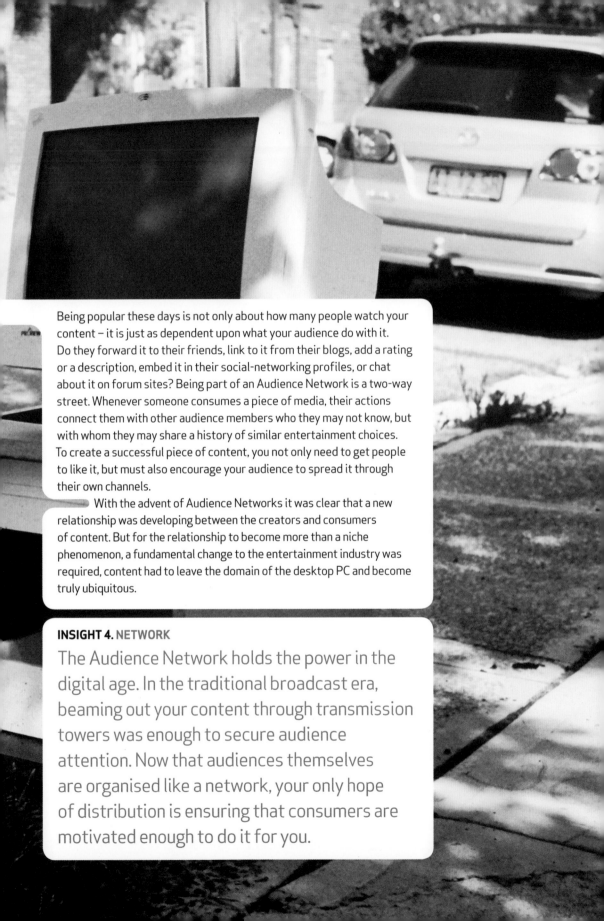

Being popular these days is not only about how many people watch your content – it is just as dependent upon what your audience do with it. Do they forward it to their friends, link to it from their blogs, add a rating or a description, embed it in their social-networking profiles, or chat about it on forum sites? Being part of an Audience Network is a two-way street. Whenever someone consumes a piece of media, their actions connect them with other audience members who they may not know, but with whom they may share a history of similar entertainment choices. To create a successful piece of content, you not only need to get people to like it, but must also encourage your audience to spread it through their own channels.

With the advent of Audience Networks it was clear that a new relationship was developing between the creators and consumers of content. But for the relationship to become more than a niche phenomenon, a fundamental change to the entertainment industry was required, content had to leave the domain of the desktop PC and become truly ubiquitous.

INSIGHT 4. NETWORK

The Audience Network holds the power in the digital age. In the traditional broadcast era, beaming out your content through transmission towers was enough to secure audience attention. Now that audiences themselves are organised like a network, your only hope of distribution is ensuring that consumers are motivated enough to do it for you.

ANYTIME

5. UBIQUITY

Putting a basketball-sized object into space might not sound like a particularly great moment in history, but picture the scene: you're sitting in a roadside diner in a mid-west American town in the late fifties, when you read in the newspaper that the Russians have just successfully launched Sputnik, the world's first artificial satellite. This was the stuff of science fiction and, more importantly, it was the start of a race that the United States was determined to win.

Within a year President Eisenhower had created the Advanced Research Projects Agency (ARPA), which was to be run by Dr J. C. R. Licklider. Dr Licklider was an unusual man who combined expertise in engineering with psychology. During the Second World War he became fascinated by how electronics could be applied to understanding human communications, which gave him a unique perspective on where computing was heading.

These days, we take connectivity for granted, but this has not always been the case.

At one time, computers were isolated objects. A computer in the mid-fifties – a behemoth, glowing with valve tubes and spitting out information drilled into punch cards – could easily have been mistaken for some kind of gigantic manufacturing device.

Licklider focused his research on investigating how computers could be linked up to form a system of communication; the result was ARPANET, the first incarnation of what would one day become the Internet. In 1968, nodes, or host computers, were established at the University of California Santa Barbara, UCLA, SRI International and the University of Utah. ARPANET grew from these small beginnings as more and more nodes were eventually added, and broadened its reach across the globe.

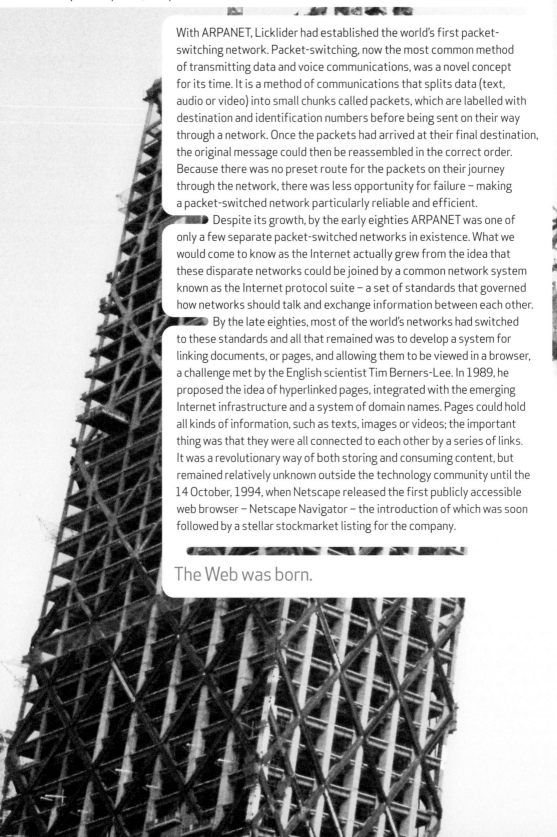

With ARPANET, Licklider had established the world's first packet-switching network. Packet-switching, now the most common method of transmitting data and voice communications, was a novel concept for its time. It is a method of communications that splits data (text, audio or video) into small chunks called packets, which are labelled with destination and identification numbers before being sent on their way through a network. Once the packets had arrived at their final destination, the original message could then be reassembled in the correct order. Because there was no preset route for the packets on their journey through the network, there was less opportunity for failure – making a packet-switched network particularly reliable and efficient.

Despite its growth, by the early eighties ARPANET was one of only a few separate packet-switched networks in existence. What we would come to know as the Internet actually grew from the idea that these disparate networks could be joined by a common network system known as the Internet protocol suite – a set of standards that governed how networks should talk and exchange information between each other.

By the late eighties, most of the world's networks had switched to these standards and all that remained was to develop a system for linking documents, or pages, and allowing them to be viewed in a browser, a challenge met by the English scientist Tim Berners-Lee. In 1989, he proposed the idea of hyperlinked pages, integrated with the emerging Internet infrastructure and a system of domain names. Pages could hold all kinds of information, such as texts, images or videos; the important thing was that they were all connected to each other by a series of links. It was a revolutionary way of both storing and consuming content, but remained relatively unknown outside the technology community until the 14 October, 1994, when Netscape released the first publicly accessible web browser – Netscape Navigator – the introduction of which was soon followed by a stellar stockmarket listing for the company.

The Web was born.

The Internet is now so commonplace that it has almost become invisible. For the same reason, you may not have noticed that the network it is based on is changing.

We were used to perceiving the Internet as a utility – something that we access when we need it. We sit down at work and look at the weather, share prices or funny videos, before going home and checking our emails on the computer after dinner. There was a concept of 'logging on' and 'logging off'.

But what if there was no off-switch and the Internet was always present? How would our relationship to content change if we were continually connected? How would it change the way in which we relate to each other?

Mobile internet access is something that Asian consumers are more familiar with; there are more mobile devices in Asia than web-connected computers. In Japan, mobile devices are the primary tool for accessing the Internet, whereas in South Korea mobile broadband is so fast and prevalent that you can download an entire movie in moments while sitting on a bus. But this is only the beginning. The gadgets in our pockets, the embedded sensors in everyday devices and the multiplying screens that surround us all form part of a growing canopy of connectivity.

Through a diverse range of new wireless standards such as WiFi, WiMax and 3G, the web of access is constantly expanding. It is now possible to tap into a wealth of media content and personal communications almost anywhere in the world.

This is a new kind of network:
a Ubiquitous Network.

Everywhere
Internet

CIVIC V

Being ubiquitous means more than simply being able to check your messages wherever you are – Blackberries provided that luxury years ago. In a Ubiquitous Network, content will sit on servers and either be streamed directly or downloaded and played back from the memory of a mobile device. These servers might be based in California, Shanghai or Mumbai, but ultimately the geographical origins of the content will make little difference to the consumer.

In fact, the most powerful features of ubiquity will become apparent without conscious action: personal jewellery that glows when people you know are nearby; umbrellas that beep as you leave your house if weather reports have indicated rain; photo frames that display images as your friends capture them on the other side of the world; or music players that endlessly fill themselves with new tracks, based on your listening preferences.

Indeed, the Ubiquitous Network is already forming. Step on any subway train in Seoul and you will see dozens of office workers and teenagers avidly watching baseball or serialized local dramas on handheld mobile devices. Their favourite content follows them wherever they are.

It's a powerful idea: any content, on any device, at any time and in any place. Your experience of entertainment will only vary in terms of what you are doing and the screens that are available to you at the time.

Traditionally, media products were designed and packaged for specific uses in certain places. Movies were viewed in a cinema while DVDs were generally played at home and movie trailers might have been streamed on to a computer or formatted into mini episodes for mobile phones.

A Ubiquitous Network will allow a far more fluid approach to how consumers can consume and interact with content.

To watch content on a large, high-definition screen with theatrical sound, consumers will access a large file with high resolution. For viewing content on a portable device, a smaller file will be provided. The important thing is that the underlying piece of content will be the same, but as media formats are simplified, the situations in which consumers can access material will expand.

Studio

Content Servers

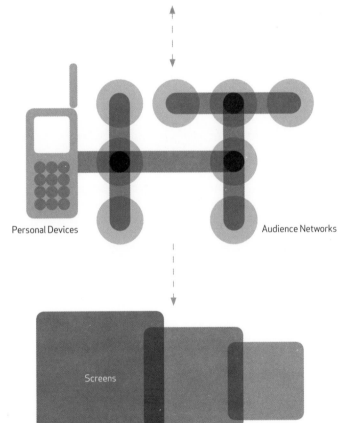

Personal Devices

Audience Networks

Screens

The Ubiquitous Network

The Ubiquitous Network has four aspects that are worth exploring.

1. CONTENT
There are basically two types of content.

Professional: anything created by professional media companies such as Hollywood studios, record labels or news networks, typically characterized by high production budgets, sophisticated merchandising and integrated marketing platforms.

Personal: media created by consumers – blogs, photos, home videos or reviews – either as original content or remixes of professional content.

Some of this content will be stored locally on home servers or portable devices, but the vast majority will sit in huge server farms in secure areas with low power costs, accessed through a high-speed wireless connection. With a fast enough connection, local device storage will be mainly used as a large cache to ensure smooth and continuous playback.

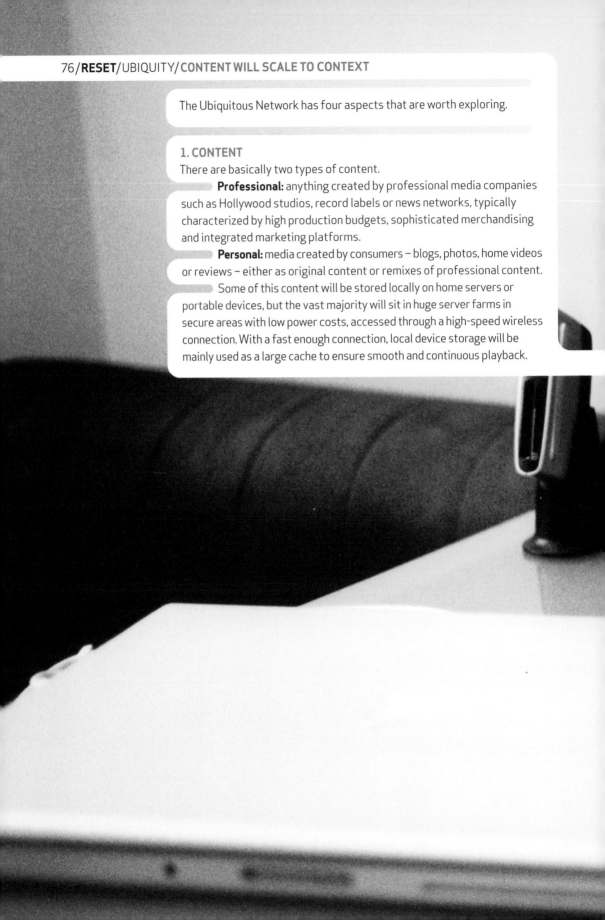

2. DEVICES

Users will interact with content using a variety of personal devices, which will perform two major functions. The first is user authentication. With the assistance of secure biometrics, such as fingerprints and voiceprints, which safely identify the physical identity of a user, portable devices of the future will allow users to access and control their private data, entertainment and personal content wherever they are. This becomes particularly important when content is no longer stored locally on their device. The second function of personal devices will be to manipulate content. Here are some examples of what these devices will do:

Control: call up a favourite song and play it as you read your email on your device screen, or connect automatically with a screen on the back of an airline seat, and direct it to continue playing a movie that you were watching at home.

Capture: take a photo, shoot a short video clip or write a blog post and immediately upload it to the network to be shared with everyone you know (as well as quite a few people who you don't).

Annotate: review, rate and annotate media content to flag up things that you may like to explore further as you consume them. This could later help to create a dinner party playlist, or a series of news items for further review and study. Importantly, the more that you annotate your content, the smarter the network will become in terms of recommending entertainment and personalizing your media choices.

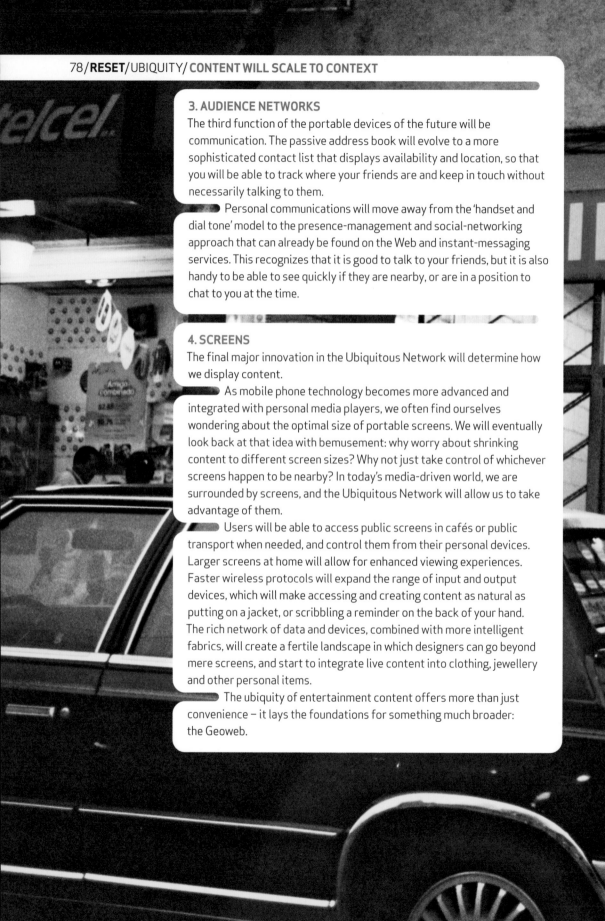

3. AUDIENCE NETWORKS

The third function of the portable devices of the future will be communication. The passive address book will evolve to a more sophisticated contact list that displays availability and location, so that you will be able to track where your friends are and keep in touch without necessarily talking to them.

Personal communications will move away from the 'handset and dial tone' model to the presence-management and social-networking approach that can already be found on the Web and instant-messaging services. This recognizes that it is good to talk to your friends, but it is also handy to be able to see quickly if they are nearby, or are in a position to chat to you at the time.

4. SCREENS

The final major innovation in the Ubiquitous Network will determine how we display content.

As mobile phone technology becomes more advanced and integrated with personal media players, we often find ourselves wondering about the optimal size of portable screens. We will eventually look back at that idea with bemusement: why worry about shrinking content to different screen sizes? Why not just take control of whichever screens happen to be nearby? In today's media-driven world, we are surrounded by screens, and the Ubiquitous Network will allow us to take advantage of them.

Users will be able to access public screens in cafés or public transport when needed, and control them from their personal devices. Larger screens at home will allow for enhanced viewing experiences. Faster wireless protocols will expand the range of input and output devices, which will make accessing and creating content as natural as putting on a jacket, or scribbling a reminder on the back of your hand. The rich network of data and devices, combined with more intelligent fabrics, will create a fertile landscape in which designers can go beyond mere screens, and start to integrate live content into clothing, jewellery and other personal items.

The ubiquity of entertainment content offers more than just convenience – it lays the foundations for something much broader: the Geoweb.

When the Web is everywhere, the way we think about content and how we access it will change. Linked by our personal devices to global server farms, we will have continuous access to personalized worlds of online entertainment and social updates from our friends. Forget prime time – media consumption will become a more perpetual experience.

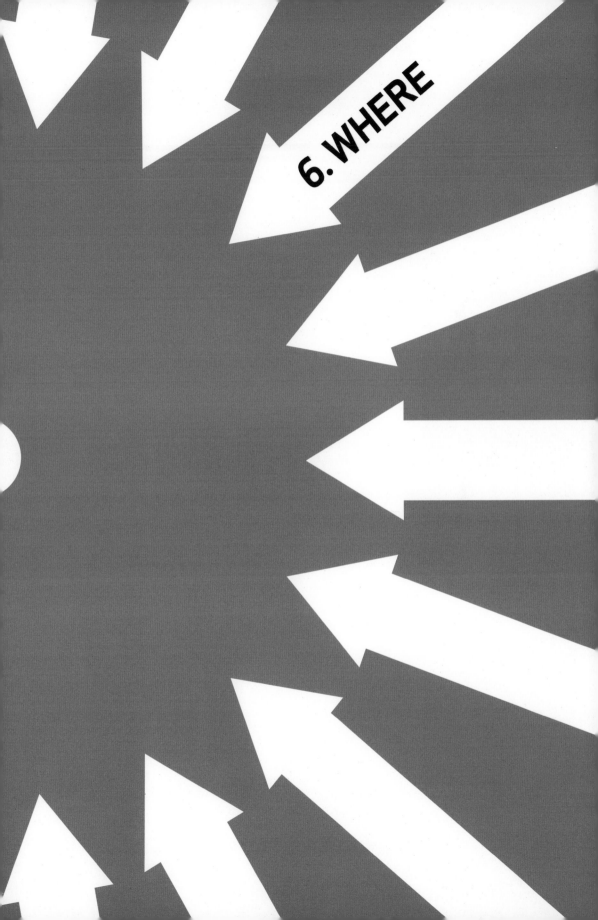

6. WHERE

You might assume that the Global Positioning System (GPS) would be a taxi driver's dream: no wrong turns, passenger disputes or consulting heavy street directories. However, this is not the case in New York City.

When city authorities tried to install GPS systems that were capable of tracking pick-up and drop-off points into driver's cars, thousands of cabbies went on strike. One group even filed a lawsuit, claiming that the units were unconstitutional. The drivers were not just annoyed about being monitored, they were afraid that the new devices would give away trade secrets by revealing their driving patterns.

Meanwhile, on the other side of the world, scientists at Sony's advanced research laboratories were also thinking deeply about tracking, but for an entirely different reason.

Most of us generate a huge amount of digital content without even realizing it: photos, messages, comments on music you have listened to, recommendations on places you have visited. So how do you identify what is important and begin to archive your memories for future reference? Jun Rekimoto, director of the Interaction Laboratory at the Sony Computer Science Laboratories, and his team came up with an interesting solution to this problem. Using a route-tracking application, they observed where a person went every day. By separating the ordinary (going to work or to the supermarket) from the memorable (holidays, a walk in the park, a day trip to another city), you could create automatic content albums based on significant days.

There is a close relationship between content and location. The places we live in, travel to or simply remember are all part of the context in which we define ourselves. In the past, we used to keep personal and fragmented records of these routes in the form of diaries, maps or lists. Someone might buy a CD while abroad to remind them of a holiday, or organize their travel photos into an online album to share with friends.

This is now changing in two ways: firstly, there is a dramatic increase in the number of consumer devices that are capable of both identifying locations and also bookmarking places for future reference. These gadgets include GPS navigation units in cars, cameras that automatically tag a physical location to a photograph, and communication devices that not only enable you talk to your friends, but let you know when they are in the area. Secondly, all of this information about people, places and objects isn't just evaporating into the datasphere – it is being recorded in a new kind of network. More importantly, this communal 'memory' is being used to arrange content into more and more meaningful contexts.

TLC DIAL 3-1-1

NE COMMISSION
06

There is a name for this new grid of location-organized content: the Geoweb.

In order to go somewhere, you need to know where you are starting from, but this can prove harder than it sounds. Early navigators used their sextants to measure latitude, but longitude remained a considerable mystery. In fact, it was such a problem that through an Act of Parliament in 1714, the British Government even offered a reward for a simple method to precisely determin a ship's longitude. The development of accurate chronometers would eventually solve the problem, but few in the eighteenth century could have imagined where the search for reliable navigation would eventually take us.

When the Russians launched Sputnik, the US military realized that the position of the satellite could be tracked by observing the radio signal that is transmitted, which increased as it approached and decreased as it left a given area. Importantly, this also meant that the same radio signals could be used to identify a person's location on the ground. This concept became the basis for the Global Positioning System (GPS), which – with twenty-four satellites – was fully operational by the mid-nineties. Next, the world needed some better maps.

Google Earth was a sensation when it first appeared. Using a range of coordinates, people could zoom in on a high-quality satellite image of a house, a beach or a busy suburban street. Naturally, the first thing that everyone did was look up where they lived. Stories began to emerge about people using the mapping software in unusual ways: relief workers coordinating their efforts in New Orleans, military analysts spotting Chinese nuclear submarines, or inspectors in Buenos Aires checking whether people were correctly reporting the size of their properties. Google even sent GPS kits to India to assist locals in creating more accurate maps of their neighbourhoods.

But what made Google Earth different to mapping systems that had come before it, was that is was a tabula rasa – a blank slate. Anyone could add their own layers of information, data and content. The detail of fixed geographic formations and buildings were possibly the least interesting part of the map; the real value was in the form of content that had been assigned or geo-tagged to specific locations. Geo-tagged data grew at an exponential rate, including photos, videos, routing data, tourism information, weather patterns, travel reviews, news reports, site histories, project developments and environmental simulation data. The new grid of information was like a thickening outer layer of content, organized by location. The region could be as small as a café, or as large as a continent.

Perhaps most importantly, the rise of the Geoweb held the possibility of changing our relationship to the delivery of content.

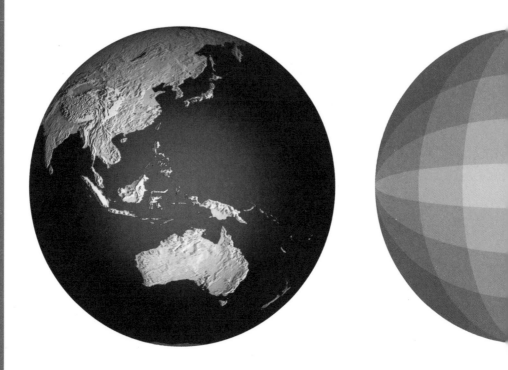

The Geoweb
Once simply divided by longitude and latitude, the world is now becoming a three-dimensional grid
of linked data.

Media companies have long been obsessed with the linear.

Broadcast platforms such as television and radio delivered programmes one after another.

Hollywood studios traditionally delivered their content to world markets in a set sequence.

Movies were delivered in a set progression, from cinemas to DVD, video-on-demand and finally TV syndication markets.

Linear distribution and geographic control were key components from the Factory era of command and control. DVDs were region-locked, video games bought in one country would not play in another, and streaming TV shows that were freely available in the United States would not play if you accessed them from anywhere else.

This is now beginning to change. Geography, and more specifically the Geoweb, is no longer a limitation, but is starting to become a catalyst for the consumption of content. For example, one of the most popular video-sharing sites in China, YouKu.com, encourages the practice of 'PaiKe' – citizen videos tagged to a specific location. PaiKe has become very popular – thousands of users now provide geographically relevant content in China from events as diverse as local festivals to commemorations of the Sichuan earthquake.

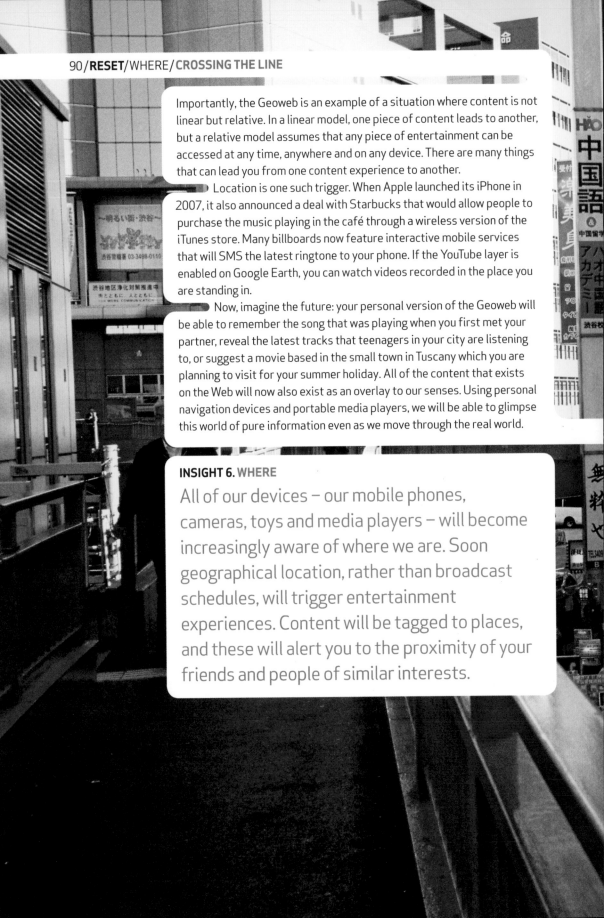

Importantly, the Geoweb is an example of a situation where content is not linear but relative. In a linear model, one piece of content leads to another, but a relative model assumes that any piece of entertainment can be accessed at any time, anywhere and on any device. There are many things that can lead you from one content experience to another.

Location is one such trigger. When Apple launched its iPhone in 2007, it also announced a deal with Starbucks that would allow people to purchase the music playing in the café through a wireless version of the iTunes store. Many billboards now feature interactive mobile services that will SMS the latest ringtone to your phone. If the YouTube layer is enabled on Google Earth, you can watch videos recorded in the place you are standing in.

Now, imagine the future: your personal version of the Geoweb will be able to remember the song that was playing when you first met your partner, reveal the latest tracks that teenagers in your city are listening to, or suggest a movie based in the small town in Tuscany which you are planning to visit for your summer holiday. All of the content that exists on the Web will now also exist as an overlay to our senses. Using personal navigation devices and portable media players, we will be able to glimpse this world of pure information even as we move through the real world.

INSIGHT 6. WHERE

All of our devices – our mobile phones, cameras, toys and media players – will become increasingly aware of where we are. Soon geographical location, rather than broadcast schedules, will trigger entertainment experiences. Content will be tagged to places, and these will alert you to the proximity of your friends and people of similar interests.

WE ARE SMARTER

TOGETHER

7. CROWD

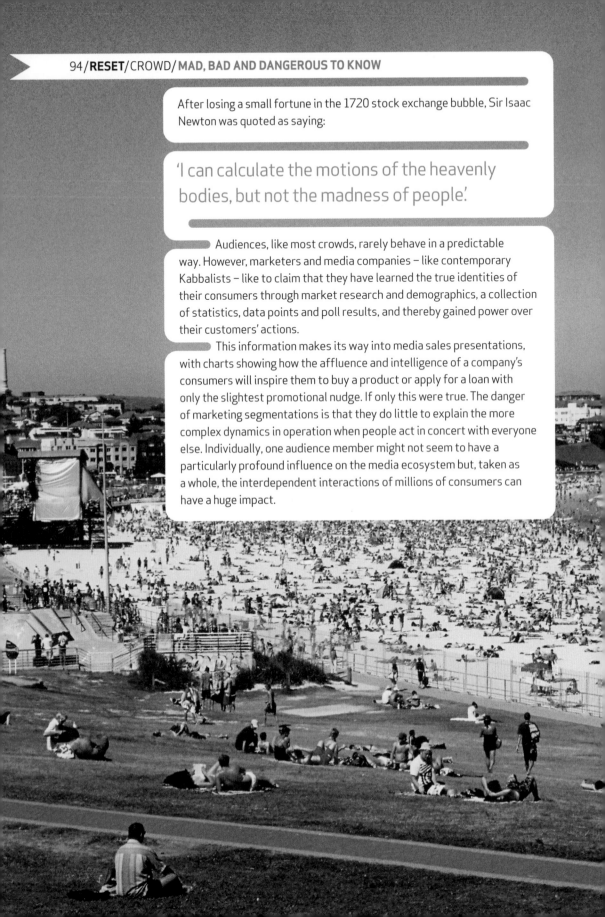

After losing a small fortune in the 1720 stock exchange bubble, Sir Isaac Newton was quoted as saying:

'I can calculate the motions of the heavenly bodies, but not the madness of people.'

Audiences, like most crowds, rarely behave in a predictable way. However, marketers and media companies – like contemporary Kabbalists – like to claim that they have learned the true identities of their consumers through market research and demographics, a collection of statistics, data points and poll results, and thereby gained power over their customers' actions.

This information makes its way into media sales presentations, with charts showing how the affluence and intelligence of a company's consumers will inspire them to buy a product or apply for a loan with only the slightest promotional nudge. If only this were true. The danger of marketing segmentations is that they do little to explain the more complex dynamics in operation when people act in concert with everyone else. Individually, one audience member might not seem to have a particularly profound influence on the media ecosystem but, taken as a whole, the interdependent interactions of millions of consumers can have a huge impact.

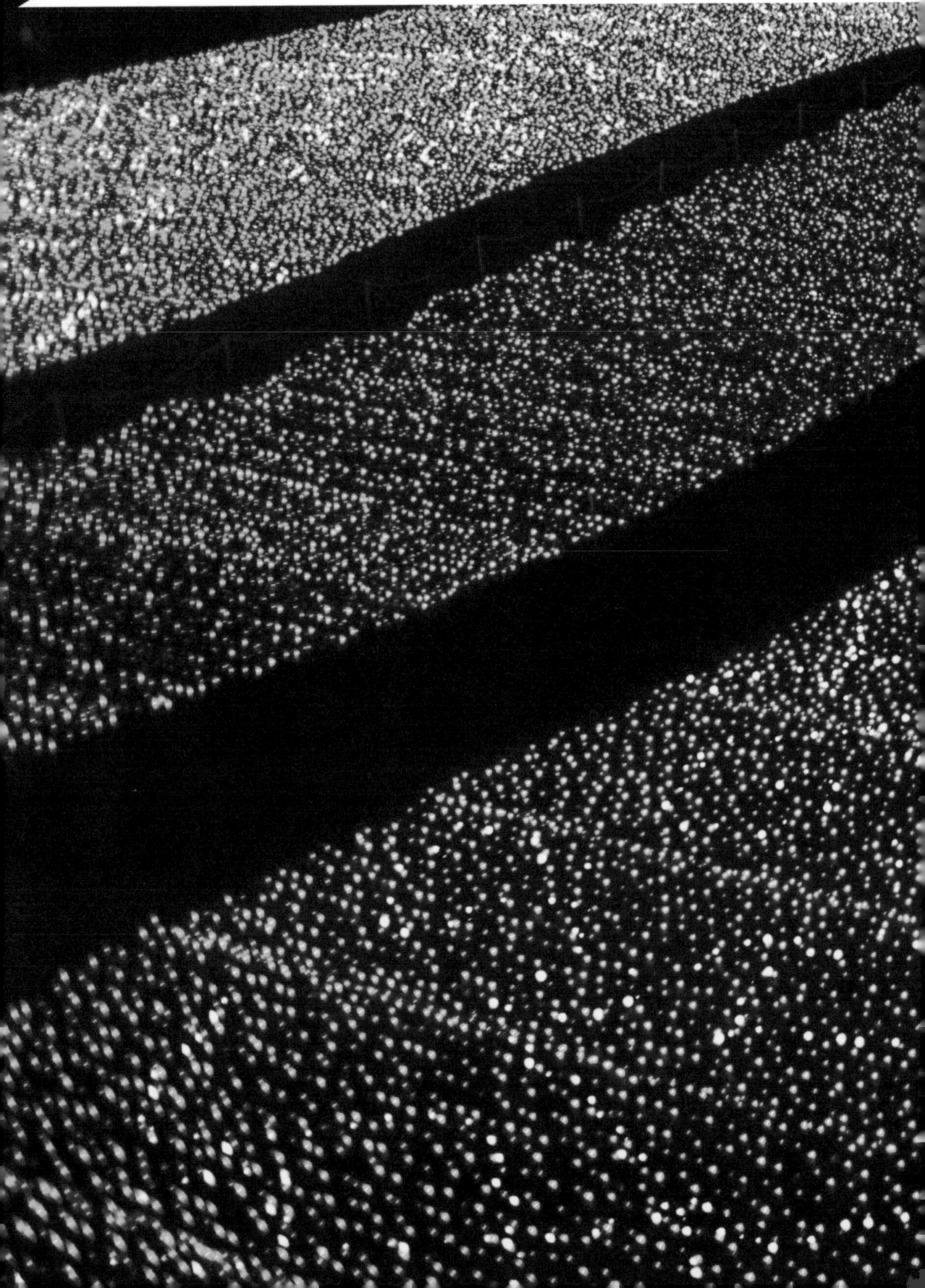

A single ant is a fragile being: a sudden gust of wind, a drop of rain or an accidental human footfall could result in instant death. An entire colony of ants, however, is a force to be reckoned with. Ants continually evolve new behavioural patterns in order to secure their survival, which biologists term as a 'complex adaptive system'. The system is complex in that it comprises multiple interconnected elements, but it is also adaptive in that it has the capacity to change and learn from experience.

The emergent intelligence of an ant colony arises from interactions between ants as they encounter each other and change their behaviour based on ingrained rules. Harvester ants, using a simple language of pheromones, can suddenly switch from building to foraging, or to looking after ant pupae, simply based on changes in the external environment. Foraging ants provide a good example of collective intelligence in action: they lay down a chemically tagged trail, and when one of their number finds food, this allows other ants to discover his path. The increasing number of trails in one area creates a stronger signal to the other ants, indicating that food has been found.

If you were to look at an individual ant, you might not consider it to be particularly clever, but by following very simple rules, the collective behaviour of a colony produces amazingly intelligent results. Although queen ants form new colonies, the collective intelligence of a colony arises entirely independently of any top-down control; in effect, no one is in charge.

The collective intelligence that can be seen in ant colonies can also be observed in the stock market, ecosystems and the human immune system or. All of these examples have a continuous process of action and reaction between independent agents, which allows the system to evolve higher forms of self-organized intelligence.

What happens next is the direct result of feedback.

The same logic of collective intelligence and feedback that breeds success in ant colonies can be applied to the millions of interactions that take place in Audience Networks. The Web is fast becoming the ultimate example of a complex adaptive system, although this has not always been the case. In its early days, the network of links was certainly complex, but it had no innate ability to learn or adapt. Hyperlinks joined websites, but unless web publishers trawled through their server logs regularly, there was no simple way for them to monitor and respond to the ebb and flow of links to and from their sites. Without feedback, collective intelligence can't function properly.

Recently, this has changed. Rather than being a random set of loosely joined documents, the Web has become a network of interconnected platforms. Feedback has become an integral part of how the Web functions and the ways in which consumers interact with each other.

– Users add comments to everything, from blog posts to podcasts and video streams, making everything on the Web part of a single enormous conversation.
– Trackbacks allow websites to link back to themselves when users discuss or comment on a piece of content.
– Photo and video sites show how many times content has been viewed, so that you can learn what is popular.
– Websites such as Digg, Del.icio.us and Stumbleupon enable audiences to rate, tag and vote for content that interests them, leading other people to the material.
– Attention-sharing services such as Twitter and Friendfeed allow users to instantly share something that they are reading, viewing or creating with their immediate circle of friends or followers.

Like ants in a colony, Audience Networks are helping to bring structure to the Web through their perpetual interaction with content.

Given the enormous amount of content that is out there, the most valuable form of structure being created by collective intelligence is relevance. This can be thought of as an expanded version of Google, which ranks the pages in its index in accordance with the number of other websites that link to a particular piece of content: every link is an indication from the masses that something is important.

The biggest question in a world of seemingly infinite entertainment choices is: 'What should I pay attention to?' The greater the number of consumers that link, rate, review, blog and discuss a piece of entertainment, the more visible the content becomes to everyone else. In a sense, all of those links are not just a sign of popularity; they form a pathway or navigation layer that helps another member in an Audience Network discover and experience that song, TV show or movie.

However, there is a risk to collective intelligence: a crowd becoming a herd. Sometimes a few individuals can have a disproportionate effect on the behaviour of a group as a whole. When people in an Audience Network pay close attention to the media-consumption behaviour of those around them, suddenly everyone can begin to imitate each other, resulting in an 'information cascade'.

Cascades can be problematic because the true value of collective intelligence is not simply creating hits, but solving the problem of personal relevance. The average of everyone's ideas of popular entertainment is not as interesting as understanding what the cross-section of people that conform to your tastes are listening to, reading and watching. So, while the *New York Times* bestseller list is interesting, far more relevant is a list of the top twenty books that your friends, or people who you consider to have good taste, are reading. As Isaac Newton realized, crowds may be mad, but their power must nevertheless begin with the actions of a single person. Like a single grain of sand causing an avalanche by falling in a particular place, minor changes in a connected system can have major effects.

INSIGHT 7. CROWD

Consumer behaviour on the Web is a complex adaptive system. A task that might be impossible for any one individual becomes a reality through the linked behaviour of online crowds. But cascading feedback also has a dark side: crowds can just as easily become mobs.

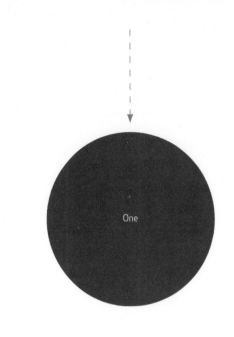

One

Many

YOU SEE
CHILDREN
PLAYING

PLA

I SEE FUTURE SOLDIERS OF THE REVOLUTION

PART 2

WHO

YOU

KNOW

IS WHAT YOU KNOW

8. SOCIAL

The first time I saw a speed-dating event, I was both impressed and somewhat disturbed. A row of men sat on one side of a line of tables, and a row of women on the other. There were a few minutes of frenetic conversation, flirtation and the occasional desperate plea, before a bell rang and everyone moved along.

It might seem implausible that anyone could make an impression in such a short time, but allegedly it barely takes any time at all. Researchers at the University of Pennsylvania studying the results of speed-dating events found that most people made their choices within the first three seconds of meeting.

Speed dating is a symptom of modernity. Despite many of us living within such a close proximity to each other, we actually meet very few people and our social circles are fairly limited. To add new links to our personal network, we need to cheat a little – which is where Rabbi Yaacov Deyo comes in. By all accounts, speed dating was his idea, as a means of ensuring that Jewish singles had the opportunity to meet each other in large cities where they were in the minority.

Of course, finding love is not the only reason that people attempt to hack their social circles. Getting a job, finding a house, organizing a party, meeting new friends or looking for a new flatmate are all activities that require us to find ways to add connections to our individual social groups. Diversity is the key – without it, no new ideas or people would ever enter our lives.

Interestingly, technology is not only making it easier to form social connections, but it is also introducing new types of relationships that have no real analogue with real-world social ties. When children talk about their friends on a social-networking platform such as Facebook or MySpace, you can be assured that they mean something very different from what an older generation understood by the word when they were growing up. On the social web, friendship is no longer a binary concept; it exists in shades of grey. By connecting to someone online, it is possible to know just about everything about them – what kind of music they like, the books they have read, who they used to date, where they have been on holiday – and yet never to have met or spoken to them.

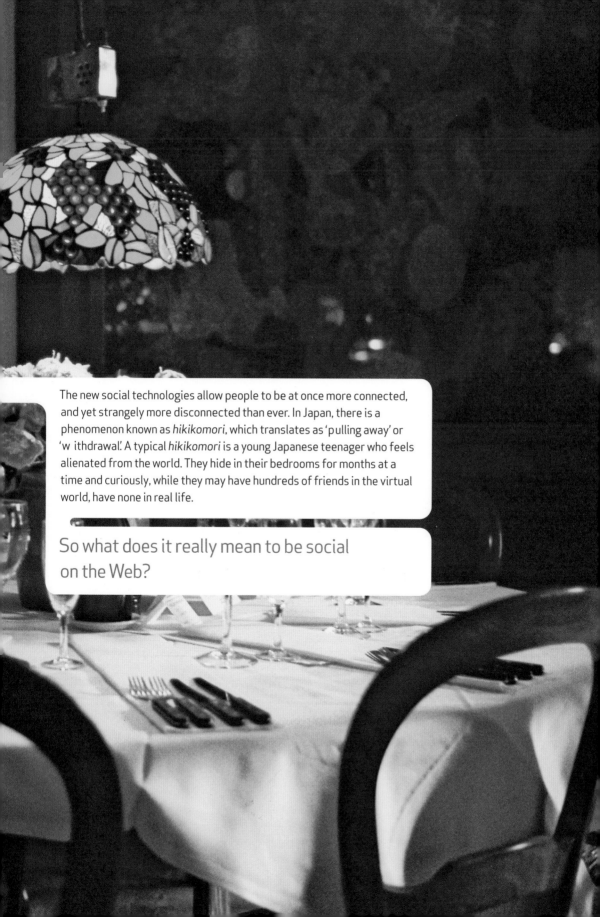

The new social technologies allow people to be at once more connected, and yet strangely more disconnected than ever. In Japan, there is a phenomenon known as *hikikomori*, which translates as 'pulling away' or 'w ithdrawal'. A typical *hikikomori* is a young Japanese teenager who feels alienated from the world. They hide in their bedrooms for months at a time and curiously, while they may have hundreds of friends in the virtual world, have none in real life.

So what does it really mean to be social on the Web?

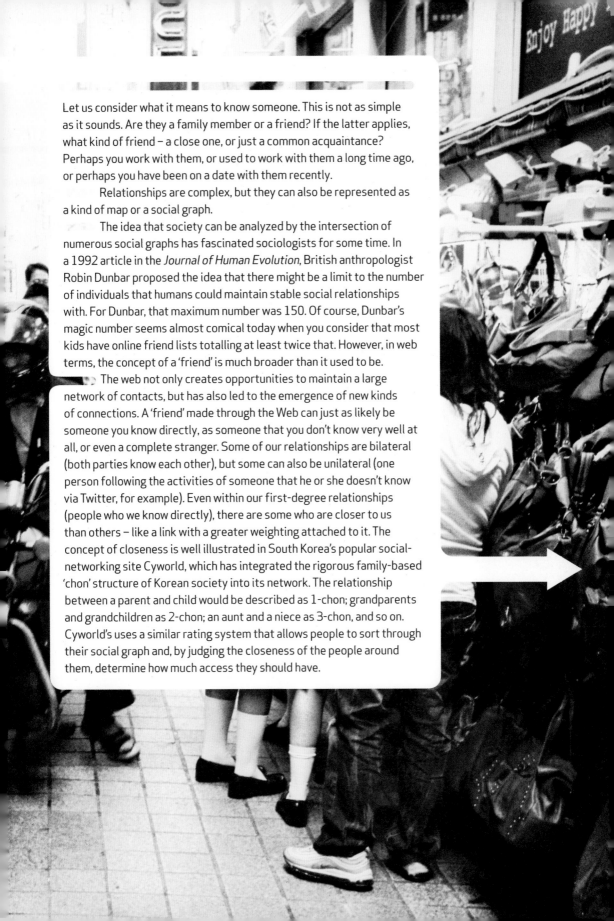

Let us consider what it means to know someone. This is not as simple as it sounds. Are they a family member or a friend? If the latter applies, what kind of friend – a close one, or just a common acquaintance? Perhaps you work with them, or used to work with them a long time ago, or perhaps you have been on a date with them recently.

Relationships are complex, but they can also be represented as a kind of map or a social graph.

The idea that society can be analyzed by the intersection of numerous social graphs has fascinated sociologists for some time. In a 1992 article in the *Journal of Human Evolution*, British anthropologist Robin Dunbar proposed the idea that there might be a limit to the number of individuals that humans could maintain stable social relationships with. For Dunbar, that maximum number was 150. Of course, Dunbar's magic number seems almost comical today when you consider that most kids have online friend lists totalling at least twice that. However, in web terms, the concept of a 'friend' is much broader than it used to be.

The web not only creates opportunities to maintain a large network of contacts, but has also led to the emergence of new kinds of connections. A 'friend' made through the Web can just as likely be someone you know directly, as someone that you don't know very well at all, or even a complete stranger. Some of our relationships are bilateral (both parties know each other), but some can also be unilateral (one person following the activities of someone that he or she doesn't know via Twitter, for example). Even within our first-degree relationships (people who we know directly), there are some who are closer to us than others – like a link with a greater weighting attached to it. The concept of closeness is well illustrated in South Korea's popular social-networking site Cyworld, which has integrated the rigorous family-based 'chon' structure of Korean society into its network. The relationship between a parent and child would be described as 1-chon; grandparents and grandchildren as 2-chon; an aunt and a niece as 3-chon, and so on. Cyworld's uses a similar rating system that allows people to sort through their social graph and, by judging the closeness of the people around them, determine how much access they should have.

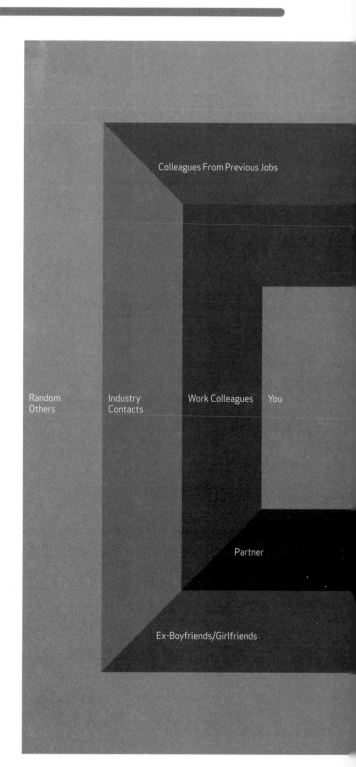

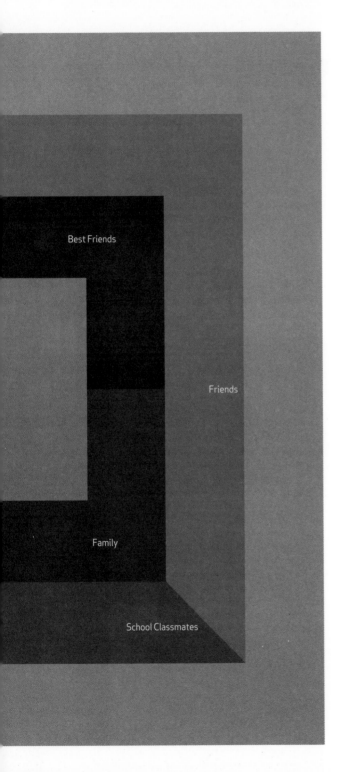

Best Friends

Friends

Family

School Classmates

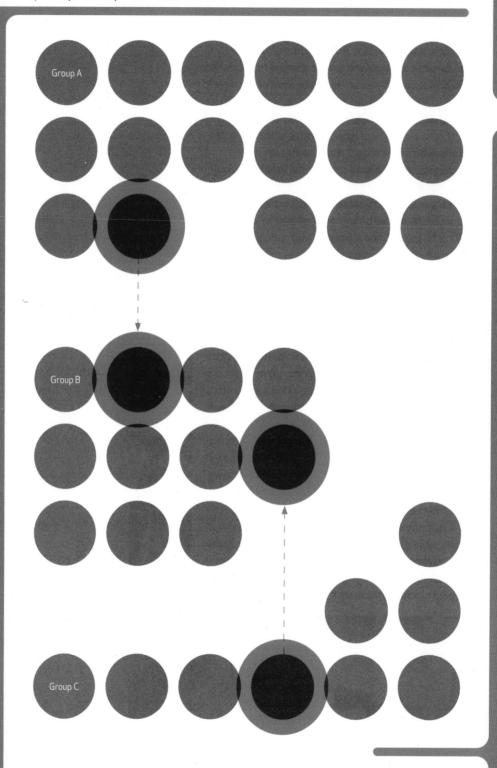

Group A

Group B

Group C

Social Connections

Although closeness is an important concept when it comes to privacy and personal content, if anything social networks thrive on weak ties. According to American social scientist Mark Granovetter, it is these loose connections that are the most valuable when it comes to finding a job, meeting a partner or even launching a new restaurant in a local area. This makes sense, as most of our close friends are likely to know each other and share knowledge. Finding new information, therefore, involves looking outside our immediate circle.

Everyone in Group A knows each other, as do those in Group B and C. The only way in which new information can percolate into these tightly connected clusters is through external links between the groups.

One of the most frequently discussed concepts in social networks is the idea that we live in a small world. In this small world, any two people are likely to be linked by a short chain of acquaintances that varies in length. This concept was famously described in the popular play *Six Degrees of Separation*, written by John Guare and first performed in 1990. The play discusses the idea that any two separate individuals on the planet can be linked through their connections with only six other people.

In the sixties and seventies, participants in small-world experiments successfully found social paths from Nebraska to Boston and from Los Angeles to New York. Originally these trials were carried out using written letters, but in a more recent experiment 60,000 individuals were able to repeat the experiment using email to form chains with just four links on average across different continents.

There is no doubt that communications technology separates our world into smaller networks. But, curiously, it also makes our small worlds more transparent. When you have forty friends on MySpace, you can not only view their pages, but also browse through those of their friends, and often their friends' friends. Similarly, when you add a friend on Facebook, you are automatically shown all the acquaintances that you have in common. The Koreans have a word for the practice of going through people's profiles, looking for other people you know: *pado*, which literally means 'riding the wave'.

Even the word 'friend' is changing. It is fast becoming less of a noun and more of a verb.

You don't make friends anymore – you 'friend' people. It's quite different.

To friend someone is to create a connection with them and to bring them into your social graph. Sometimes you may know them personally, but often it is purely based on someone's photograph, user name, interests or the style in which they have created their profile page.

When people connect their social networks, they open up a wealth of information about themselves, including what they are doing, what they are watching and other people they know. The more people lead digital lives – taking pictures, updating status messages, writing blog posts – the more the simple act of virtual friendship becomes closer to being a subscription to all the content created by that person. In a way, everyone has become their own media company.

Unsurprisingly, the opposite also applies. When you block someone on a social network, you are literally making yourself invisible to them. You will no longer appear in search queries that person might make about you and they will not be able to see any content you have created, nor will you be able to see them or what they are doing. It is as if you have both been deleted from each other's virtual universe.

The act of adding or blocking people on social networks has become an entirely new form of behaviour, with rules of etiquette as subtle and nuanced as any real-world form of interaction. As American social futurist and researcher Danah Boyd has observed, the organization of friends on your networking profile is a kind of identity performance. Friending is part of the way in which the next generation of consumers like to represent who they are and what they like doing. It is as much about creating an image as it is an indication of true social connection.

This leads to an interesting point: the reason for creating your social graph is not only to capture the people already known to you – it is the opportunity it provides for access to people you don't know that is truly valuable. Networks are vital sources of information, full of insights about what is going on in your world, opportunities and, as we shall see, discovering new forms of entertainment.

INSIGHT 8. SOCIAL

Being social online means more than just socializing. On the Web, being someone's friend no longer necessarily implies a tie of familiarity or affection. Social networks have evolved from a simple tool of staying in touch to a more complex infrastructure for sharing status updates, common interests and media content.

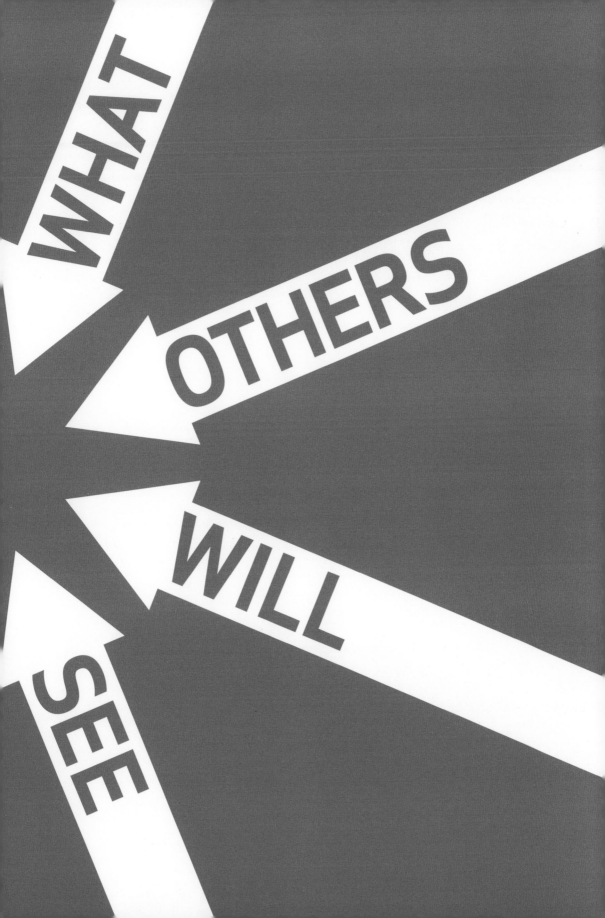

Walter Annenberg was a mid-twentieth-century American billionaire. He made his money in publishing during the golden age of advertising, entertained the likes of Ronald Reagan, Frank Sinatra, Bob Hope and Bing Crosby at his Palm Springs ranch, and used his media influence to rattle the cages of governments and politicians. But perhaps his biggest success of all was the creation of the listings magazine *TV Guide* in 1952.

For over fifty years, *TV Guide* was a national institution. It was often the only publication that a generation addicted to television read. As Homer Simpson once quipped, the modern-day Three Rs are 'Reading *TV Guide*, Writing to *TV Guide* and Renewing *TV Guide*'.

But then things changed. The problem was not that *TV Guide* was a magazine or that people weren't watching as much television as they used to; it was the ways of watching that had changed. With the increased availability of Personal Video Recorders such as TiVo, DVDs and web-delivered content, no one was really paying attention to the official broadcast schedules anymore.

Before long, our children will look at us strangely when told that we used to consult a weekly publication to see what shows were broadcast at a particular time. It will sound as quaint to them as someone today saying that they used to watch the news at a cinema or speak to an operator to connect a phone call. And yet the irony remains: with infinite amounts of content at our disposal, it has become more important than ever to have some guidance in making entertainment choices. So where will this guidance come from in the future?

The answer is the same as Jean-Paul Sartre's infamous definition of hell: other people.

Sometimes it is a bit creepy when machines know too much about you. There is a story that American Express once had a call centre that linked its database with the caller ID details, so that the operator would know who was on the line and could answer using the caller's name: 'Yes, Mrs Jones, what can I do for you?' Naturally, customers found this somewhat disconcerting.

While it is useful when machines help you, it can be alarming when they try to second-guess you. One TiVo user had his programming schedule automatically filled with a series of very camp TV shows after his set-top box misinterpreted his wife's consumption of cooking and lifestyle shows as an indicator of his sexual preferences. The machine had been programmed to recognize cooking and lifestyle programming as appealing only to women and homosexual men.

Entertainment platforms today are full of complex algorithms: Amazon observes your book and CD purchases, Netflix tracks the movies that you rent, iTunes scans the contents of your music library. The idea is that by comparing your choices with those of like-minded people, all of these services can do a better job of making new recommendations for you, and thereby sell more products.

This method of recommendations revolves around a technique called 'collaborative filtering'. It works by making predictions about the interests of a single user by analysing taste information collected from many users.

In a way, collaborative filtering works on the same principles as the networks that we have been exploring in previous chapters. Every time you make an online purchase, that information links you into a network of consumers with similar tastes to you. If nothing else, making suggestions about related products is a clever retail merchandising strategy. Unfortunately, sometimes the uncanny accuracy of recommendations is itself a problem. You will often find that the suggested albums, movies or books are ones that you already know about or own. What you really want is to discover content that is outside your immediate experience, but would still interest you. Achieving that requires a more sophisticated approach to gleaning insights from social networks and shared media consumption.

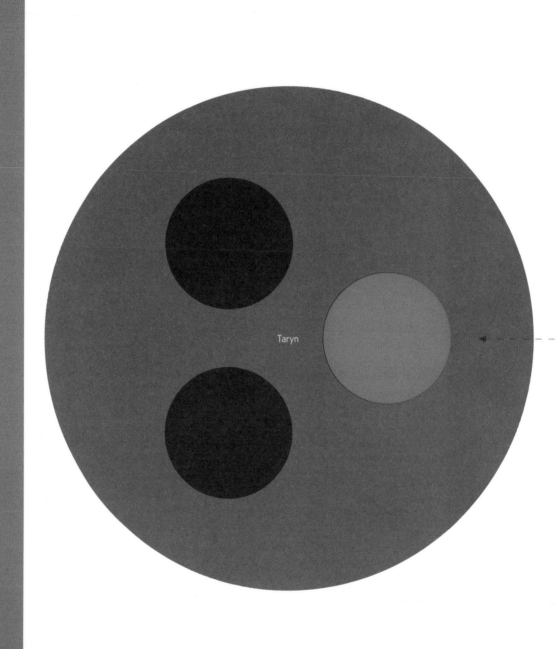

Taryn

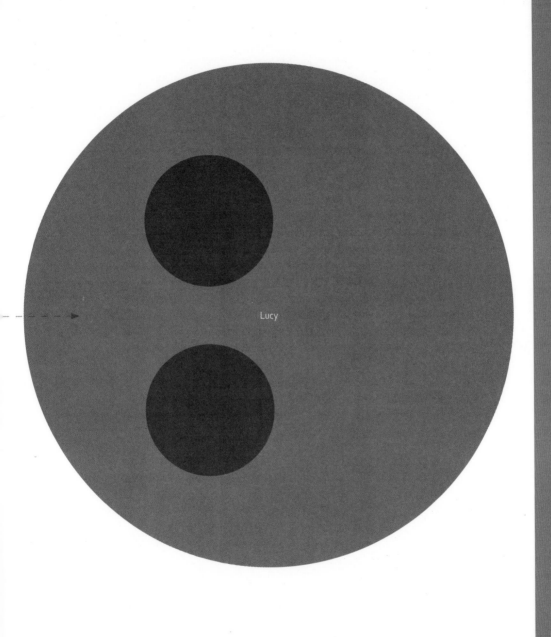

Lucy

A Tale of Two Tastes
Let's assume that Taryn has bought three songs from a music retailer, as in the diagram. If Lucy already has two of those songs in her collection, it seems highly likely that she would enjoy the other song that Taryn has bought.

The best entertainment experiences have always been social: laughing at a TV sitcom with your family, going to the movies on a date, listening to music with friends at a party. However, the joys of being social were all but forgotten by our technology for a few years. Glance out of the window and you will see people walking down the street with headphones in their ears, blocking out the world – but it wasn't meant to be that way. If you look at the design of the original Sony Walkman, you will notice that it had two headphone jacks, and a button allowing users to talk. The real magic of media is when it connects us.

Imagine watching a TV series and seeing a row of photo icons on the right side of the screen, representing all of your friends who are also fans of the show. You would be able to see the comments other audience members have made on it, their favourite scenes and what else they are watching. Or you could be walking down the street listening to your personal music player, with your social settings set to open; an alert will sound if someone nearby has similar musical tastes to you. You have never met, but in a way you are already in the same Audience Network.

In another scenario, when you get home from work each night you check your recommendation list of new entertainment content to watch. It is a programming guide of sorts, but not one written by a professional scheduler or a media company – it's a live feed of items that have been watched and then reviewed by a small group of entertainment jockeys (EJs) that you trust and subscribe to. You trust their opinion in the niche areas that they track, and the content they select is automatically tagged for your consumption wherever you are. You can already observe the beginnings of this trend in the rise of music and video blogs that curate the best entertainment content on the Web, often providing these recommendations as a live stream which audiences can listen to.

We are moving away from the early phase of recommendation engines, based on abstract observations of consumer behaviour, to platforms that make Audience Networks more transparent. The difference is subtle but powerful. Consider this example: instead of receiving a recommendation from Amazon after adding a book to your shopping cart, you were shown links to the last ten people who had also bought that book (and who consented to sharing the information). Clicking on them would let you see all of their other purchases. You could even subscribe to them as a feed, so that you would be informed when they bought something else, and could elect to have the item sent to you as well.

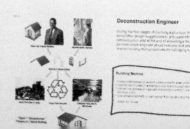

Audience Networks are powerful for the very reason that they are made up of real people, not just aggregated results from an algorithm. In 2007, the US TV Network CBS bought a company called Last.fm for US$280 million. Last.fm uses software to track what kind of music people listen to, either on their computers or on their personal music devices. This information is then transferred on to a user's profile page, allowing the service to make recommendations of both related music and other people with similar tastes.

As the Web becomes more social and more applications are created that are able to track the relationships we have with each other and with content, it will become easier for us to share our entertainment preferences. Some of our referrals will be deliberate: we will forward things that we discover to our friends or anyone else that might be interested. But our most influential recommendations will be shared unconsciously, through the simple act of consumption. In doing so, there is a good chance that in the future we will not watch anything that has not been referred to us from our own social networks.

INSIGHT 9. DISCOVERY

Traditional programming is at an end. In the future, the most valuable source of recommendations about movies, TV shows, music, books and games will not come from programme directors, channel managers or magazine editors, but from people in our own social networks.

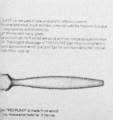

10. VIRAL ONE

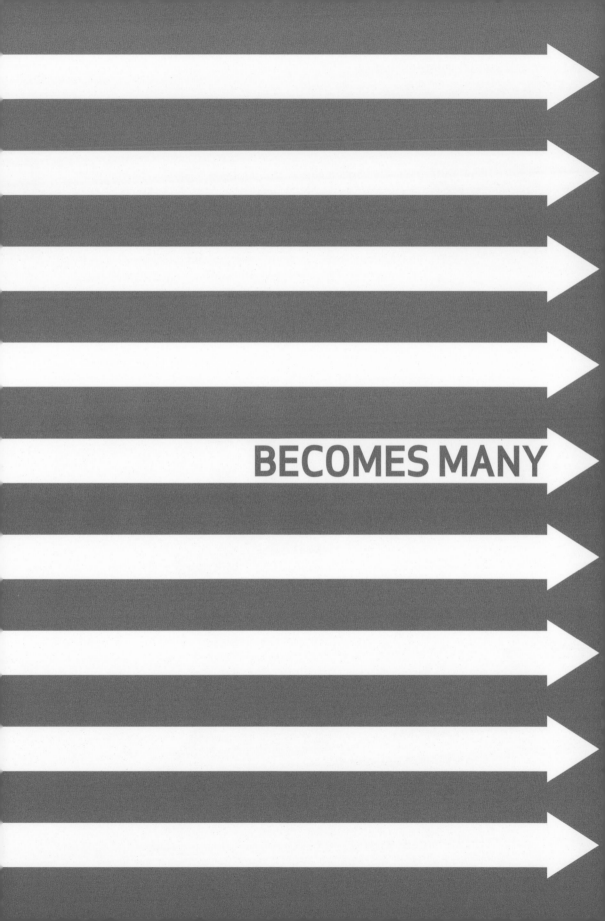

BECOMES MANY

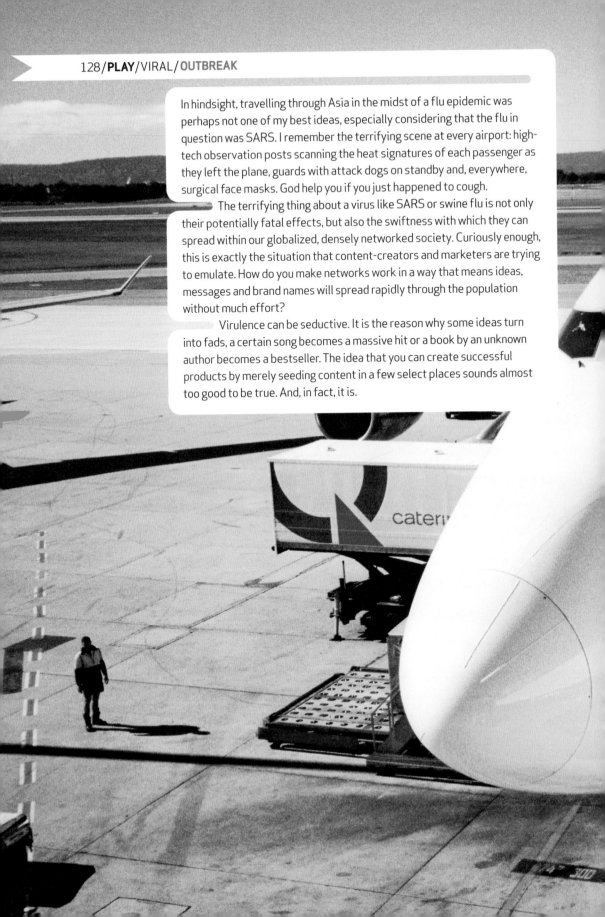

In hindsight, travelling through Asia in the midst of a flu epidemic was perhaps not one of my best ideas, especially considering that the flu in question was SARS. I remember the terrifying scene at every airport: high-tech observation posts scanning the heat signatures of each passenger as they left the plane, guards with attack dogs on standby and, everywhere, surgical face masks. God help you if you just happened to cough.

The terrifying thing about a virus like SARS or swine flu is not only their potentially fatal effects, but also the swiftness with which they can spread within our globalized, densely networked society. Curiously enough, this is exactly the situation that content-creators and marketers are trying to emulate. How do you make networks work in a way that means ideas, messages and brand names will spread rapidly through the population without much effort?

Virulence can be seductive. It is the reason why some ideas turn into fads, a certain song becomes a massive hit or a book by an unknown author becomes a bestseller. The idea that you can create successful products by merely seeding content in a few select places sounds almost too good to be true. And, in fact, it is.

There are really two schools of thought concerning viral distribution. On one hand you have Malcolm Gladwell, a staff writer with *The New Yorker* and author of the bestselling book *The Tipping Point*, first published in 2000.

Gladwell argued that the key to making ideas spread quickly is to find the right handful of super-influencers to get the ball rolling. In Gladwell's view, picking a small selection of highly connected people is the first and most important step to creating a viral impact. He called this idea the 'Law of the Few'.

Australian social scientist Duncan Watts, however, disagrees; he believes that network effects are too complex to be reliably reproduced by targeting only a handful of influential individuals. Ideas do spread virally, but how fast this happens depends on whether or not everyone is easily infected. If everyone is susceptible, then anyone randomly infected can start an epidemic, rather than just the highly connected few.

In a sense, both Watts and Gladwell are right. How fast something becomes viral depends upon both how infectious the carriers are and how susceptible the population is to being infected. This concept was captured in a mathematical model devised by the Scottish physician and epidemiologist Anderson Gray McKendrick and his colleague William Kermack to explain the rapid rise and fall in the number of infected patients observed in plague and cholera epidemics. In their model, known as SIR, people could be in one of three possible states during an epidemic:

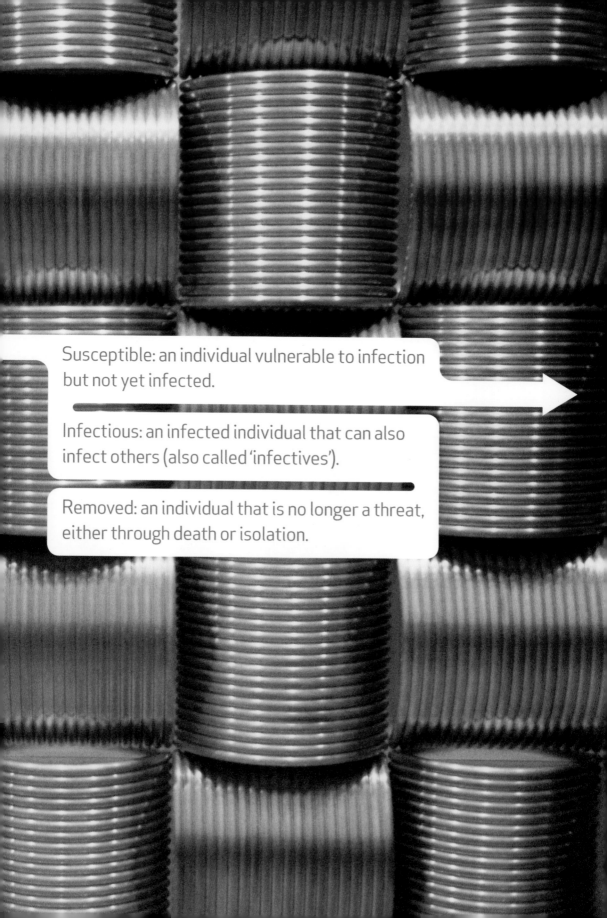

Susceptible: an individual vulnerable to infection but not yet infected.

Infectious: an infected individual that can also infect others (also called 'infectives').

Removed: an individual that is no longer a threat, either through death or isolation.

Epidemics occur as the infectious encounter the susceptible, like in a zombie film. In the beginning, there are relatively few infected individuals, so the overall rate of new infections stays low, but this gradually increases. The key to preventing an epidemic is to prevent it from reaching the explosive growth phase, when the rate of growth of new infections spirals out of control.

Of course, there are many killer viruses that burn themselves out in isolated villages and never bring civilization to its knees; the reproduction rate – the average number of new infections created by each currently infected individual – is not the only factor. In isolated communities, while the reproduction rate may skyrocket within the small social network, there is no link to the outside world. But if a highly infectious victim met an outsider who then returned to his own community, that would be a different story.

This is the viral equivalent of a social short cut, and it gives us an important clue as to how little sparks become bush fires. Using short cuts, a virus is able not only to move within a local network, but to take paths between network clusters. In this way, a loosely connected network of individual clusters can become one globally connected component.

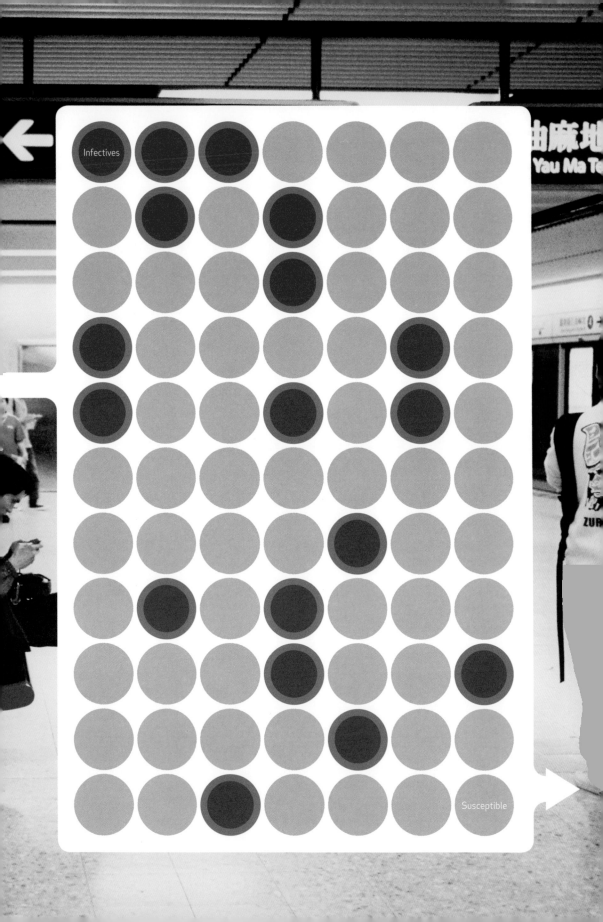

It is an amazing phenomenon. Physicists call it percolation and would insist that we have witnessed a phase transition, whereas sociologists would observe that a community has just formed. Entertainment executives, on the other hand, have a different phrase for it: a 'breakout hit'. They will lean back in their leather chairs with an excited if confused smile, as their under-financed, out-of-the-blue, destined-for-failure project becomes the new summer blockbuster.

Cluster 1

Cluster 2

Super Distribution occurs when content or an idea infects not just one cluster, but a whole network of loosely connected social networks.

To understand how cluster-connecting links form, we must return to the matter of how susceptible random groups of people are to infection. As sociologists like to point out, people are more likely to be influenced into doing something if increasing numbers of people around them are doing it: this leads to an information cascade.

Cascades happen when people start imitating others' choices rather than making their own. As the author James Surowiecki points out in his 2004 book *The Wisdom of Crowds*, if a group of people are standing on a street corner looking upwards, more and more people will join them. Merit doesn't really come into it; people will assume that if other people are doing something, there must be a good reason. Of course, imitating without thinking can be embarrassing. You could end up with a crowd looking aimlessly at a patch of empty sky.

One of my favourite experiments in this area was conducted by Duncan Watts, who in 2006 created a simulation involving music fans. Watts set up an online music-downloading service filled with real but unknown music. Some of the subjects taking part in the experiment were asked to rank songs without reference to what other people thought, while the others were put into groups where they could see how other members were ranking the songs.

Not surprisingly, when people could see what others were doing cascades took over. Some songs became very popular and others drifted to the bottom. The really interesting thing was that in each of the groups where the subjects were allowed to rank songs, none of the same songs became hits; this showed that although people were influenced by each other's behaviour, the final result really depended on which songs were voted up early on, rather than how good the song actually was.

That implication for entertainment content was clear: early visibility is a crucial factor that determines ultimate popularity in a networked environment.

If the viral spread of new entertainment products is essentially random and not controlled by a small handful of individuals, how do distributors increase their chances? The answer is Super Distribution – in other words, seeding your content in as many socially volatile patches as possible.

In the glory days of the Factory, distribution was tightly controlled. You released your content on certain platforms, in certain areas and at certain times; to do otherwise would have been financial suicide. Super Distribution is the exact opposite – the more widely and freely your content is dispersed, the higher the chances that it will find enough receptive consumers early on and trigger a viral avalanche.

The lesson of Super Distribution was a difficult one at first for the TV networks. When their shows began to appear on YouTube or peer-to-peer file-trading networks, they struck back with lawsuits. But gradually they realized that if they didn't encourage consumption on as many platforms as possible, not only would people continue to do it anyway, but they were also missing out on a golden opportunity. YouTube employed digital identification technology, which made it very simple for copyright owners to identify when a user had uploaded one of their shows. Rather than deleting their illegally uploaded content immediately, the media company could elect to keep the file intact with all of its social connections, blog links and community commentary – and simply share the advertising revenue that accrued from viewership of that clip with YouTube.

Of course, getting people to do your dirty work for you isn't guaranteed. Super Distribution relies on individuals and how they interact with other, which is very different from the traditional model of blanketing the airwaves and street corners with mass advertising. In order for a new show, song or entertainment product to go viral, a sufficient number of individuals and clusters have to forward, embed, discuss and engage with the content on their personal networks. Whether or not this happens, and how it reflects on the product, depends heavily upon how the consumers think people will respond to their recommendation behaviour.

Jure Leskovec, Lada Adamic and Bernardo Huberman, researchers at Hewlett Packard Labs, performed an interesting study on the ways in which ideas spread through recommendation networks. They found that, unlike a normal epidemic, most recommendation chains terminate after just a few steps. In other words, the transmission of a social virus gradually decays. As a person sends out more and more recommendations for a certain product, after a certain point the success per recommendation declines. The logic behind this is that individuals have influence over a few of their friends, but not everybody they know.

When you start thinking about the significance of personal brands in recommendation networks, you realize that viral distribution is a two-way communication loop. What you send out contains as much information about you as it does about the content or product you are recommending. For example, what are your impressions of a friend who forwards on a legitimate appeal for charity fundraising in comparison to someone who emails you a patently obvious banking scam as if it were a great moneymaking opportunity?

Social networks have a memory. Like the brain reinforcing a strong memory association, every time someone in a network forwards something that people find funny or useful, those links become stronger and bolder. In a similar way, someone who continually forwards irritating or irrelevant material will be forming strong links, albeit of a more negative kind. If you want the next generation of media consumers to become your distribution network, you have to value the impact on their personal equity. When you take into account social virus decay, you realise that the most important brand is actually the person recommending the product or service, not the recommended brand itself.

INSIGHT 10. VIRAL

Content, like a contagion, spreads through Audience Networks by harnessing the links between people. The more random the connections between social clusters, the better the chance that a piece of media will achieve Super Distribution. However, the underlying logic of virality is very different to traditional marketing. It is not enough to merely persuade someone to pay attention. They have to be motivated enough to risk their own personal brand by becoming your advocate.

A random series of numbers, a small furry creature with purple ears, the forty-third Susan at Hotmail or simply anonymous: there is no such thing as simply being yourself online. How we describe ourselves, our visual images, symbols and actions, and the content we create are all part of a personality composite that sits between ourselves and the rest of the world. The author Kurt Vonnegut said it best in his novel *Mother Night*:

'We are what we pretend to be'.

Assuming an online persona is a fast-growing trend. Today, there are virtually no entertainment platforms that do not require consumers to create a profile of themselves at one level or another, to describe what they like, who they know and what they do. The more time we spend online, the more important it becomes for us to invest time and energy into developing online personas that best represent us. Or at least represent how we want to be seen.

It is tempting to view social profiling as a market research tool, but this is not necessarily the case. When people describe themselves for other people to see, this inevitably presupposes a choice of character and becomes a game of identity performance. In simple terms, it creates a mirror to our actual selves: an avatar.

In Hindu philosophy, an avatar is an incarnation of a higher being on earth. The Sanskrit word *avatāra* literally means 'descent' and usually implies a deliberate plunge into lower realms of existence for a particular purpose. The gods used their avatars as a skin when they needed one. Consumers do the same.

Early video games were purely kinetic – you shot things, hit things and got out of the way of things. As games became more complex and developed perspective, it became the norm to assume a character, such as an Italian plumber, an athletic hedgehog or a manic monkey. The suspension of disbelief that came with donning a game persona was just as important as the necessary eye-hand coordination, if not more so.

Now the trend is personalization; in multiplayer games such as 'World of Warcraft' users customize their own characters, imbuing them with strength and experience – and this is only the beginning. Eventually these personas will roam freely between a range of worlds and adventures. Nintendo's hugely popular Wii console already invites its players to create their own characters, which are then superimposed on to a number of its game titles. Online platforms, from multiplayer games to music retailers, are encouraging consumers to invest time in creating elaborate digital identities – the idea being that if people leave more of themselves online, they will come back more often.

Creating game avatars is not just a frivolous exercise. Powerful characters with significant game experience are a valuable commodity. Digital personas and items sell on the black market for thousands of dollars. Virtual gold farms have developed in parts of Asia, where indentured workers spend hours logged on, creating digital characters to sell online. In 2007, eBay actually banned the auction of virtual items, delisting all property related to virtual worlds and online games, citing legal complexities over the actual ownership of such items.

The exchange of virtual items is an interesting point of cultural difference between the West and the East. Although many gamers in the West see the development of characters, the gaining of points and experience levels as a matter of personal skill, it is very common in the East to simply 'buy' your way into a game by using money to instantly start off with a more powerful avatar. In fact, because of this, an increasing number of multiplayer games in Asia are becoming free, subsidized by features that allow you to pay to upgrade your character, or to replay an unsuccessful fight scene with more powerful weapons and life points.

But the really interesting thing about all of this is that games are only one of the many entertainment products that will involve consumers in the act of identity production and exchange. One of the major differences between older and younger users on the Web concerns their degree of comfort with multiple personalities and user identities. Younger users are happy to assume a variety of online identities, they will happily level cities as a killer robot via one persona, while chatting in five simultaneous chat windows in the guise of various others.

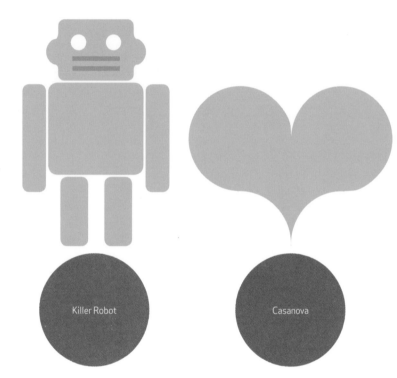

Killer Robot

Casanova

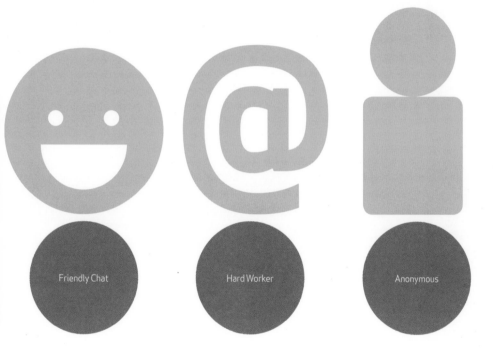

Friendly Chat

Hard Worker

Anonymous

One Person, Many Faces
The new generation are adept at handling multiple online identities.

Every culture handles the issues of identity production in its own way. In the West teenagers using websites such as Friendster and MySpace are often quite open about their real names, lives and personal activities, whereas in parts of Asia users are more likely to hide behind virtual identities. Many Asian societies have embraced social networking but tend to be more comfortable with a pretext of anonymity. Not surprisingly, then, Asian consumers are inclined to eschew real profile pictures for those of animated manga characters. Internet users in China are more than happy to represent themselves on chat programs such as QQ with a simple six-digit number. Many Chinese children are capable of reeling off a dozen of their friends' number codes as easily as reciting their real names.

The South Koreans, on the other hand, favour their anime personas – media that are easily lost in translation. The 'mini-me's' on social networking site Cyworld were so uniformly cute and cherubic that when the site launched in the United States, they had to be toughened up and expanded to include other cultures. A further contrast is presented by social networks in Japan. Here, one of the fastest growing mobile communities in Japan is a network called Mobagetown. Unlike the Japanese social networking site Mixi, which has a strict invitation-only system and a focuses on building online communities for friends who already know each other in the real world, Mobagetown forbids members to make requests to meet up in real life. Role-play is a key dynamic in users' engagement with one another in the Japanese mobile community. There are 'Mobaboyfriends', 'Mobagirlfriends', 'Mobafamilies' and 'Mobaschools'. Among the chatrooms there are virtual restaurants where members pretend to order and serve food, classrooms where virtual school is held and host-bars where male hosts listen to the troubles of female 'clients'.

Gender, as you might expect, is a flashpoint for conflict. Male gamers in Asia are often focused on creating digital personas that they like to look at, rather than worrying about how other people see them in the game world. As a result, some popular multiplayer games in China, such as 'King of the World', have started banning males masquerading as female characters. Anyone who chooses to play as a female in the game has to prove their gender using a webcam. It's a problem not unfamiliar to Internet users in the West. On 'Second Life', entire subcultures are devoted to the etiquette of 'furries', or people who enjoy playing non-humans or animals.

Being yourself has never been so complex.

Closely related to the growth of avatars are virtual currencies, which are generally used to purchase upgrades to enhance or decorate a consumer's online personality. QQ coins were originally developed by the Chinese social-networking platform Tencent to pay for services on their social media platform QQ, such as electronic greeting cards, online games and anti-virus software. But when this virtual currency exploded in popularity, the Chinese government was not amused. QQ coins were part of an entire parallel economy in virtual items. Paying a few QQ coins could enable you to add decorations or clothes to your avatar, or to perform an amusing practical joke like turning your friend's profile into a pig. These coins could be purchased with a bank, telephone or 'QQ' card at an official price of the equivalent to US$0.15, which is where the problems started.

Because of the lack of online credit card facilities or other e-commerce alternatives in China, QQ coins started to become a monetary substitute for all manner of unrelated transactions. In fact, the QQ coin became so widespread that Chinese banking officials speculated on its impact upon the stability of the national currency. Xinhua, China's official news agency, reported cases of people earning thousands of yuan per month by trading in QQ coins, which had suddenly become the currency of choice for all manner of black-market online activities, including gambling and money laundering.

QQ had actually got the idea of selling QQ coins from South Korea. The largest online social network in South Korea, Cyworld, had long operated its own virtual currency, called dotori, or 'acorns'. One acorn costs the equivalent of US$0.08. For a time, almost every teenager in South Korea had their own 'mini hompy', a personal home page that the user would customize in an endless competition to outdo everyone else. Popular users – generally pretty girls – would often find themselves deluged with acorn gifts from other users hoping to win favour. You would be surprised at the total of all that acorn trading added up to: by all accounts, at least US$300,000 per day in digital sales during 2006.

There was a certain irony to all of this. At a time when so many social networks in the West were desperately trying to come up with advertising-based business models that kept them profitable, social platforms in Japan, South Korea and China were making so much money from the sale of virtual items that they barely needed to worry about even selling advertising space.

INSIGHT 11. AVATAR

The more we live, work and play online, the more important it will be that we invest in the way we represent ourselves online. Avatars are not just virtual characters – they are our digital doppelgängers. In the same way that a well-equipped online game character can be worth thousands of dollars in resale, our online identities can have serious consequences for our own perceived value – whether in our professional or personal lives.

WE DESIRE TO LIVE

12.LIFECAST

LIVES

OTHERS

EACH

George Eastman, the founder of Kodak and inventor of roll film, was not one for complexity. With the slogan 'you press the button, we do the rest', he put the first camera into the hands of consumers in 1888. Eastman's view was that the secret of turning photography into a mass-market activity was to simplify the cumbersome and complicated system of processing, developing and printing. So that is what he did, and for the next hundred years or so, despite improvements in technology, the basic elements of taking photos and having them printed did not really change.

Consumers bought rolls of film, exposed them in their cameras, dropped the used cartridges in for processing, paid for photo prints, obtained doubles to share photos with friends and spent hours pasting their best works into photo albums or mounting them in slide brackets for after-dinner slide-shows.

But digital cameras introduced entirely new ways of interacting with photos, and the behaviour of consumers changed. Rather than shooting a set amount of photos and having the whole roll printed, people began capturing thousands of images, deleting some, sharing hundreds and then maybe printing a few. The shockwaves resulting from these changes created major problems for a number of traditional film companies. Some, like Agfa and Polaroid, never recovered.

The death of film was a game-changer, but the real game had barely begun.

Is it possible never to forget anything? Computer pioneer Gordon Bell thought so, and was willing to give it a try.

Gordon Bell is no stranger to technology. He oversaw the development of the VAX minicomputer, a milestone in the development of minicomputers and, as a researcher at Microsoft since the mid-nineties, he has had access to the scientific equivalent of serious toys. So, for the last ten years, everything Bell has done has been digitized, catalogued and stored in his digital archive: every message, photo and phone call made; every web page visited; any instant-messaging exchanges conducted; labels from bottles of wine consumed; as well as countless small scraps of paper and other random items. But this isn't all.

Every morning when he leaves his house, Bell places a small device around his neck. It is a small camera programmed to automatically take pictures at regular intervals. The idea is that with continuous capture and enough storage, you can backtrack through the archive of your life as if it were a gigantic memory cache.

Bell's inspiration came from the former head of the US Office of Scientific Research and Development, Vannevar Bush. At the end of the Second World War, Bush wondered what his scientists would do now that they no longer needed to invent brilliant new weapons, which led to his famous essay 'As We May Think', published in 1945. Bush foresaw radical innovations in photography, with enthusiasts wearing miniature devices the size of walnuts that captured images continuously. But he also realized that the dramatic increase in content created by individuals had serious implications for the storage and retrieval of data. To solve the problem, he imagined a new device, which he called a Memex, or memory extender. A Memex would consist of a desk with slanting translucent screens, on which a huge amount of material could be saved, retrieved and recalled. Bush's ideas were prescient; consumers were limited by the mediums that they used.

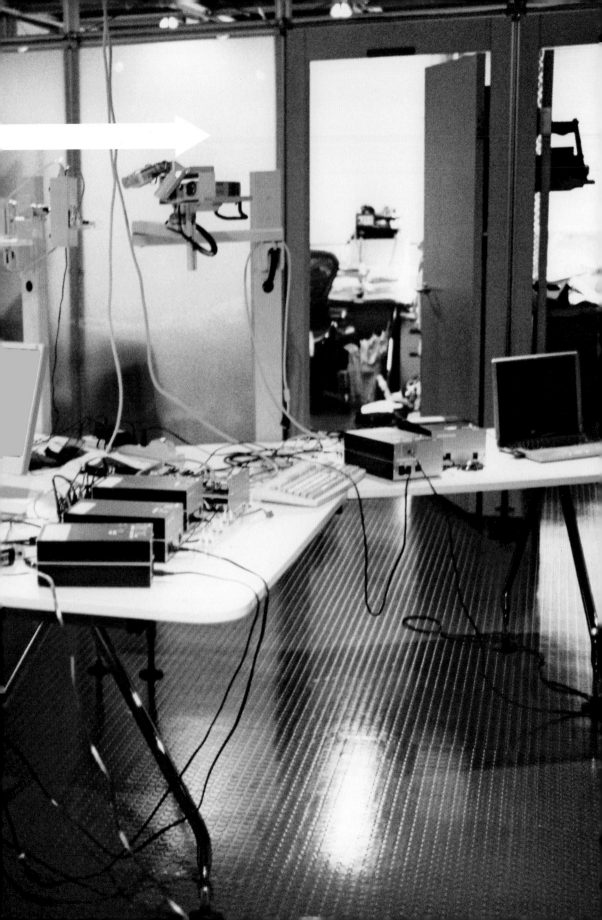

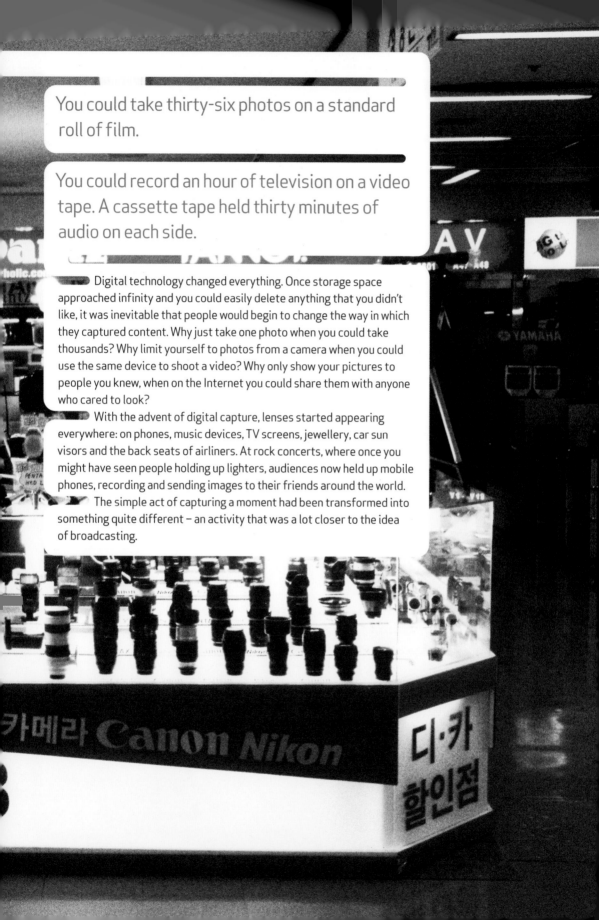

You could take thirty-six photos on a standard roll of film.

You could record an hour of television on a video tape. A cassette tape held thirty minutes of audio on each side.

Digital technology changed everything. Once storage space approached infinity and you could easily delete anything that you didn't like, it was inevitable that people would begin to change the way in which they captured content. Why just take one photo when you could take thousands? Why limit yourself to photos from a camera when you could use the same device to shoot a video? Why only show your pictures to people you knew, when on the Internet you could share them with anyone who cared to look?

With the advent of digital capture, lenses started appearing everywhere: on phones, music devices, TV screens, jewellery, car sun visors and the back seats of airliners. At rock concerts, where once you might have seen people holding up lighters, audiences now held up mobile phones, recording and sending images to their friends around the world.

The simple act of capturing a moment had been transformed into something quite different – an activity that was a lot closer to the idea of broadcasting.

Justin Kan, an unassuming 23-year-old Korean-American Yale graduate, was an unlikely candidate for fame. However, in early 2007, he decided to attach a bag full of computer and broadcasting equipment to his back, and wear a cap with a video camera fixed to it. He was no longer just Justin; broadcasting every moment of his life continuously to the Internet, he was Justin.tv.

An unlikely fan base gathered to watch Justin's ordinary life, whether he was taking a girl on a date or dealing with the San Francisco Police, who turned up at his apartment after his online fans had called in a false report about a stabbing. The latter event started a trend – the following day, someone reported a fire at Justin's apartment and six fire trucks immediately responded.

It was not the first time that someone had broadcast themselves. Jennifer Ringley, an attractive but otherwise unremarkable teenager, created a popular website in 1997 called Jennicam, for which she left her desktop webcam running day and night. But the easy availability of wireless technology a decade later made a big difference; it meant that people like Justin could broadcast wherever they were.

Justin was not alone. Celebrities soon got in on the act as well. After a sold-out concert at New York's Gramercy Park, teen rock band the Jonas Brothers visited a record store in Times Square. Fans went crazy, not least because every moment was captured and shown live on JonasBrothers.tv, a channel on the newly expanded Justin.tv platform. More than 110,000 people watched. It was the beginning of a trend called Lifecasting.

The special thing about Lifecasting is not the nature of the content that people are making, but the way in which it is shared. When someone Lifecasts, they transform the node they occupy in everyone's social graph into a mini-broadcast transmitter.

Of course, some nodes are more powerful than others. At 2:13 Eastern Standard Time on Friday, 17 April, 2009, Hollywood celebrity Ashton Kutcher became the first individual to attract a million followers on Twitter. In doing so, he narrowly beat CNN's breaking-news feed, which had 998,239 followers at the time. Speaking on 'Larry King Live' the next day about his duel with the world's largest news organization, he observed:

'We now live in an age in media that a single voice can have as much power and relevance on the Web, that is, as an entire media network. And I think that to me was shocking.'

Twitter's 140 character text messages are just a start. Soon Lifecasters will begin using their networks to beam out every aspect of their lives in inconceivably high definition. Recalling Gordon Bell's memory experiment, the things that people look at or read, places they travel to, friends they talk to and content they watch can be recorded and shared with everyone else. Through Lifecasting, the ultimate in first-person narratives, an element of voyeurism is undeniable. This is the same quality that has made reality TV shows such a hit for the last decade – the opportunity to peer into someone else's life for a few moments.

The spread of Lifecasting in the coming years will be aided by web-connected personal devices with highly intelligent visual recognition tools. There are already cameras that automatically take pictures when the people in view smile, and video cameras that turn themselves on when they detect motion. Software like Qik allows mobile phones to be used as personal live-broadcasting cameras which upload images in real time direct to the Web.

Of course, not everyone is destined for exhibitionism. Many people will elect to share a real-time feed of what they are doing to a select group within their social circle – and even then, maybe only involving certain highlights. But there is also no doubt that, in the future, the most famous teenager in the world will not be a product of a packaged pop group or the Hollywood Studio system; they will simply have the nerve and ambition to show the world, through a miniature wireless camera, what any party-mad eighteen-year-old sees every moment of the day. And, terrifyingly, everyone will feel compelled to watch.

INSIGHT 12. LIFECAST

The future of reality television is actual reality. Armed with persistent recording devices, access to wireless broadband and global distribution through personal social networks – tomorrow's celebrities will make their lives available 24/7 by directly broadcasting to their fans.

Lifecast Node

Lifecast Network
In a Lifecast Network, thousands or potentially millions of other people
subscribe to content broadcast live from someone else's life.

LIFE = CHANGE

13. PULSE

People are drawn to change. It's obvious really: why would you go back to look at something unless there was a possibility that it might have shifted, been expanded, or be new in some way? Look at any website, perhaps even your own, and imagine the parts that stay the same are blue, whereas the parts that change are red. How much is coloured in red?

A predominantly red page is a wonderful thing; it's never the same and is hard to predict. The rate of change is a kind of pulse, or heartbeat. In the connected world, a fast pulse is exhilarating, and it draws a crowd. You can't help but look – the fear of missing something is palpable.

People often make the mistake of designing pages for the Web that resemble elegant, unmoving statues – a frozen moment in time with perfect copy, design and navigation: the homepage as a monument.

In fact, web platforms are more like intricate machines: you decide the basic rules and then set them into motion. The magic lies not in the mechanics but in the momentum.

What attracts people to web content today is different from what worked ten years ago. People spend less time visiting the websites that they know, and more time discovering content through social platforms. Part of the reason for this is connected to the pulse; if you follow the heartbeat of the content that is being discussed in your circle of social contacts, you will tend to consume the media items that are surrounded by the most energy, conversation and feedback. This online version of conversation is very different to the mode of data retrieval from an information archive, a system on which many sites were based in the early days of the Web.

Digg.com is a good example. Created in 2004, initially as an experiment, Digg allowed its users to submit and vote on media stories that they thought were interesting. The website grew rapidly, attracting millions of users. Specific categories for topics such as technology, entertainment and science were added soon after the site's launch. In a sense, the front page of Digg enabled readers to become news editors, allowing them to prioritize items on the day's news agenda. But, of course, that was also a problem. Most of the early adopters of the site had fairly similar, technology-focused interests, which skewed the results that appeared on the front page of the service, making it less appealing to mainstream users. Nevertheless, it was a clear illustration of how a simple voting tool, powered by an Audience Network, could be a more effective interface with the world's newspapers and content sites than their own home pages. The reason for that was simple: it was driven by feedback.

Biofeedback was a popular experimental therapy technique in the late sixties. The idea was that if you could reflect the details of a person's physical state back at them, they might learn to start controlling bodily functions, such as heart rate, blood pressure, skin temperature and muscle tension. With time, it was hoped that we might be able to will ourselves to be more creative by changing the patterns of our brainwaves, or heal ourselves without resorting to drugs. Like a lot of things from the sixties, you probably had to be there to make sense of it, but the basic premise was powerful: feedback is self-reinforcing.

This is an interesting phenomenon to consider. It is one thing to acknowledge the vitality of the pulse of a web platform, and it is quite another to understand the process behind this dynamic interface. If you look closely at web traffic patterns, you can observe significant activity clusters around the areas of sites where users are providing feedback to each other.

If you submit photos and videos to a community site, the first thing you will check every day is how many people have looked at your content, and what they have said about it.

If you are going to pick a blog post to read, you are likely to choose the one with the most comments and views on it.

If you are part of a social-networking platform, it is hard not to look constantly at a page that summarizes everything your friends are doing and saying, especially if that concerns you.

It also shouldn't come as a surprise to learn that by facilitating feedback, you are encouraging the development of the parts of a web platform that change the most. In fact, a clever content platform operates as a kind of 'feedback accelerator'; it funnels and collects the community's response to your content, which in turn encourages you to create more material, which then attracts a bigger response, and so on.

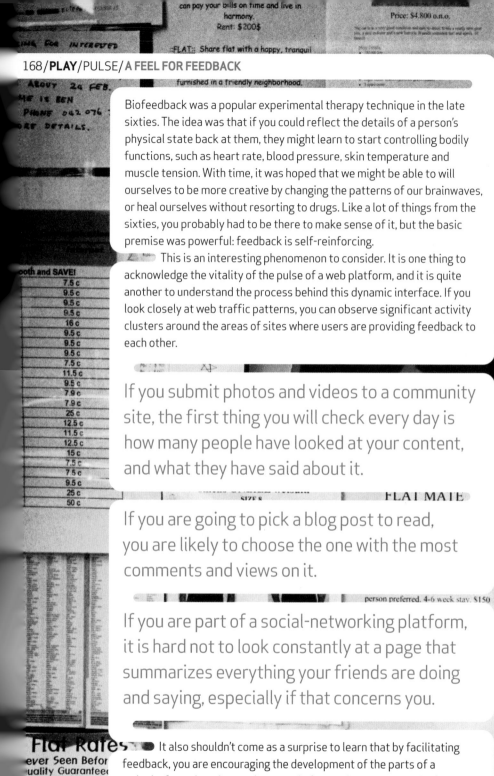

When biologists look at the mystery of why ants and bees are not particularly intelligent creatures as individuals, but collectively coordinate their effots to achieve incredible results, they find that feedback plays a significant role. No single ant knows how to make an anthill. Anthills emerge from thousands of simple interactions of ants responding to stimuli, which in turn feeds back into new interactions. The stock market works in the same way. No one individual decides what level the Dow Jones or FTSE 100 index should be on a given day. Share prices emerge from millions of decisions made by investors. When the market crashes, it's a positive feedback loop where individual actions to sell influence others around the world to do the same.

You can also view the discovery and consumption of media as a complex adaptive system. If you look at individual consumers their decisions about what to watch or read might appear random, but when viewed collectively a strange kind of order emerges. What becomes popular is often arbitrary, but that popularity is self-reinforcing.

You can learn a lot by watching what is driving the pulse of a media platform. Content creators can work out the kind of material that stirs people into action. Marketers can study the ways in which people discover content, share it and react to it. But be warned: feedback never leads to proportional results. Connected audiences are hypersensitive and differ markedly from the traditional marketing model, which is what scientists might call a determined system. A car, for instance, is a determined system: take your foot off the brake and the vehicle rolls forwards, pull the steering wheel to the left and the car follows, step on the gas and the car goes faster, and so on.

Networked media will not give you the luxury of knowing the outcome of your actions; it is extraordinarily unpredictable. The results of placing content online can vary dramatically; perhaps no one will notice you exist, or you might wake up to find that your blog post is one of Digg.com's top stories, attracting an unprecedented response that brings your server crashing down.

INSIGHT 13. PULSE

On the Web, nothing stands still. Like ants or bees, millions of online users interact within a dynamic system that is driven by feedback. The more we watch, the more others see. The more we create, the more we connect with others. The pulse of the digital revolution is change.

WE WANT TO BELIEVE

14. AUTHENTIC

I've always loved newspapers. There is something organic and tactile about them. Even as you read them, entropy sets in: sections fall out, pages rip and the ink rubs off on your fingers. I especially love the photographs – grainy and stark, the images are made up of dots large enough for you to see the white spaces in between. Grain seems to be a kind of truth; in all their roughness, newspaper photos somehow seem more real than glossy, digital images. It is an odd paradox: the lower the quality, the higher the believability – as if low resolution were a proxy for authenticity.

The very same thought occurred to me when web videos first started to become popular. Part of the magic of the early days of YouTube was that it seemed real: there were no slick Hollywood production values. For that reason you could believe that the pretty girl talking to the camera actually existed – or not, as it would turn out.

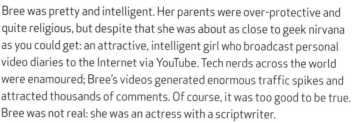

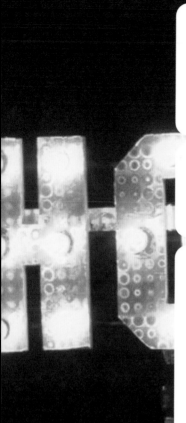

Bree was pretty and intelligent. Her parents were over-protective and quite religious, but despite that she was about as close to geek nirvana as you could get: an attractive, intelligent girl who broadcast personal video diaries to the Internet via YouTube. Tech nerds across the world were enamoured; Bree's videos generated enormous traffic spikes and attracted thousands of comments. Of course, it was too good to be true. Bree was not real: she was an actress with a scriptwriter.

Before long, user suspicion led to a collective crusade that involved analysing IP addresses, trademark filings and web-server records until the truth of the hoax was revealed. Some people called the experiment art, but most just saw it as fraud. The bottom line, however, was that even after the truth came out, audiences continued to watch. Like any great piece of entertainment, people wanted to believe in it.

However, the concept of authenticity on the Web is more complicated than something that merely appears to be real. Being authentic is about talking in a direct tone of voice that suits the connected nature of the medium. Although written a decade ago, *The Clutrain Manifesto* was eerily prescient of the importance of authenticity in web communications. The authors of the book – Rick Levine, Christopher Locke, Doc Searls and David Weinberger – argued that the Web was unlike traditional media because it enabled people to hold 'human to human' conversations. Although the writers focused on the need for corporate marketing to shift away from broadcasting half-truths about products and services, and favour more direct, honest communications instead, their argument also raised the wider issue of the ideal format of Internet content.

The rise of video-sharing websites and user-generated content has given audiences a taste for raw, unedited reality, in which immediacy and relevance surpass the impact of high production values. In the same way that reality television has transformed the TV programming market, over the next few years we are likely to see more true reality programming, that is, programmes based on actual life experiences rather than theatrical versions of reality. Why watch 'Survivor' or 'The Apprentice' when you can watch real clips of people actually doing things away from the restrictions of a sound studio? We will be watching actual people climbing mountains or searching for undersea treasure, in situations where leaving the show has more fatal consequences than on current TV programmes.

The emergence of celebrities will also change. One of the first celebries of the Internet era, Paris Hilton rose to fame through the viral distribution of her Internet video, but maintains her visibility through traditional media channels, such as newspapers and television. As greater emphasis is placed on true life experiences in the process of sharing online content, her successor will be just an ordinary girl with a wireless video device, whose exploits will be directly beamed out in real time to her own vast Audience Network.

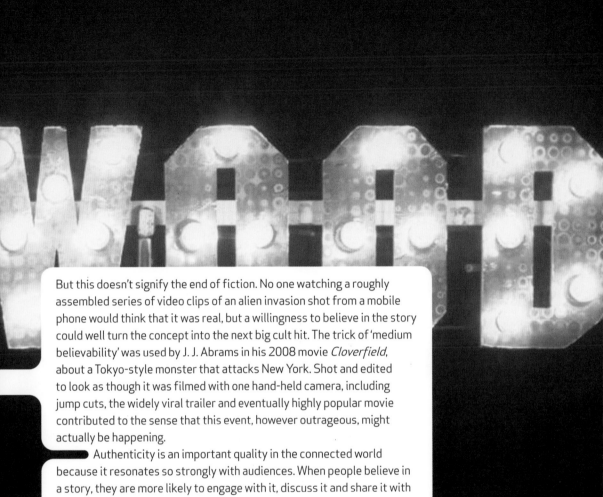

But this doesn't signify the end of fiction. No one watching a roughly assembled series of video clips of an alien invasion shot from a mobile phone would think that it was real, but a willingness to believe in the story could well turn the concept into the next big cult hit. The trick of 'medium believability' was used by J. J. Abrams in his 2008 movie *Cloverfield*, about a Tokyo-style monster that attacks New York. Shot and edited to look as though it was filmed with one hand-held camera, including jump cuts, the widely viral trailer and eventually highly popular movie contributed to the sense that this event, however outrageous, might actually be happening.

Authenticity is an important quality in the connected world because it resonates so strongly with audiences. When people believe in a story, they are more likely to engage with it, discuss it and share it with their friends. It is not as hard as it sounds. After all, being real is not the same as being realistic.

INSIGHT 14. AUTHENTIC

In an era of digital manipulation, reality is a fluid concept. When anything can be faked, nothing is presumed to be real. So what makes something authentic in the new world is not how it looks, but rather how connected it is to the underlying social fabric. In the broadcast era, actors talked to you from the screen. In the network era, you can talk back to them.

15. TAG

TO NAME
IS TO FIND

The Argentinean writer Jorge Luis Borges would have been pleased. I bought a copy of *Labyrinths*, his wonderful collection of stories, in a ramshackle old bookstore. Inside, nothing was in order: books were collected in random assortments, and the towering stacks of spines looked like they might collapse on top of you at any moment. It was, in short, heaven, and not unlike Borges' own short story 'The Infinite Library', where the narrator is confined to a vast library in which all the books that have ever been written, or ever will be written, are stacked along labyrinthine pathways. The inhabitants of the library seek a rumoured index, which holds the key to understanding their world.

A good index, as any librarian knows, is a rare find. In a speech at the O'Reilly ETech emerging technologies conference in 2005, author Clay Shirky put it succinctly: to classify things well, you have to be part mind-reader, part fortune-teller. Melvil Dewey, born to a poor family in upstate New York in 1851, gave it his best shot.

Dewey's invention, the Dewey Decimal System, attempted to organize all the world's knowledge into ten main categories that, excluding the first class (000: Computers, information and general reference), proceeded from the divine (philosophy and religion) to the mundane (history and geography). The problem with Dewey's magic numbers was that no matter how clever a taxonomy of subjects you come up with, the chances are you will never keep pace with the speed at which people develop new ideas – or the words they use when searching for them.

Fortunately, the Network had a solution of its own.

Tagging is an online activity where audiences describe content in their own words. It lies at the intersection between two of the Web's prevailing search philosophies: human editing and organic search results.

In the early days of search engines, Yahoo took up the task of classifying the entire Web, using the company's own human editors. It worked well at first, but with every passing year the huge volume of new websites made the task seem more daunting and increasingly futile.

Google's riposte was timely: forget humans, use an algorithm. But, although this was effective, Google's search results didn't solve the problem of classification. Search for a 'mustang' and you might get a car, a plane, a horse or a model of Fender guitar. The problem was not just ambiguity, but the fact that you couldn't really get a sense of how content was described.

However, what if every piece of content you found also displayed how it had been described by other people? This would be a useful signpost to finding more of what you wanted. The photo-sharing site Flickr decided to give it a try. Users could label either their own or other people's pictures with descriptive tags. Although any one user might only label a handful of photos, the combined descriptive behaviours of a large user base generated a remarkably effective classification system.

Rather than forming rigid categories, tagging facilitates the same kind of overlapping associations that the brain uses. So, for example, a Flickr photo of a baby might be tagged as both 'baby' and 'cute', allowing for either word to be used as a search term. This is a bottom-up approach to labelling, which has the very real advantage that the terms people are inclined to use to describe something match those that others are most likely to use when searching. With millions of photos described by millions of tags, there is a good chance that someone will have picked a word that you are considering using in a search phrase. The resulting hierarchy of tags is sometimes referred to as 'folksonomy'.

Fortunately, when it comes to tagging, people are also very effective at collectively solving large classification problems. At the beginning of 2008, the Library of Congress announced that it was going to upload 3,000 archive images to Flickr. The photos, a small fraction of the 14 million images in the archive, were part of a pilot project to see whether audiences could assist with adding descriptions and tags, as well as identifying scenes and individuals depicted in the photos. The descriptions added by users were at times quirky and at other times moving, but were almost certainly more engaging than if a lone professional historian had attempted to sit down and research each of the images individually.

Picture the scene: a young boy lays out a trail of Reese's Pieces to lure an ungainly extra-terrestrial out of a closet. This might not have been the most profound moment in cinema, but it was certainly one of the first and most successful examples of product placement, as well as a handy metaphor for a tagging trend.

Photos are not the only items to be tagged in the media world. Like the candy trail in *E.T.*, Internet users take advantage of tags and social bookmarking services such as Del.icio.us to create a content-consumption trail that they or others can follow at a later date. Whether it is a news article or a video, a tag serves as a way of reminding yourself where the content you like is located, and how to find it when you want it.

Whereas in the past consumers might have saved newspaper articles, podcasts or videos directly to their computer, they now simply post a reference to the page on a networked service that allows them to share that content with other people. Bookmarking is not only a great way to keep track of your content, it is also a means to connect with people of similar tastes. If you stumble across another user who likes books on Tuscan cookery and music by Elton John, as you do, you can subscribe to their bookmark and tagging activities as a feed, and be informed of all their consumption decisions in real time.

In the future, tagging and bookmarking will be a feature that will be integrated into most entertainment platforms. If you hear a song playing on the radio or at a nightclub and want to tag it for later purchase, you will be able to do so with your mobile device. If you are watching a movie at the cinema and see a trailer for another film you would like to see, you will be able to set an alert for when the movie is released. One step ahead of the crowd, Karl Lagerfeld, the celebrated fashion designer, has a collection of more than seventy iPods that are filled with new music by a trusted professional DJ. By all accounts, Lagerfeld listens to the tracks and tags good songs for use in parades and events.

In the future, consumption and annotation will become inseparable. Our portable devices will contain rating and tagging tools that will allow us to bookmark and describe media content, while the expanding Geoweb will enable us to place those annotations into a physical context. Imagine a world in which everything is constantly layered with the traces of people who have gone before you.

Like watching the commentary track on a DVD, you could choose to tune into past patrons' comments on the best items from the menu in a café you have just entered, elect to listen to the soundtrack that someone has chosen for looking at paintings by Monet in the Louvre, or watch a video of the fun times your friends had in the same nightclub that you are now revisiting.

Tagging will become a kind of mark-up on reality.

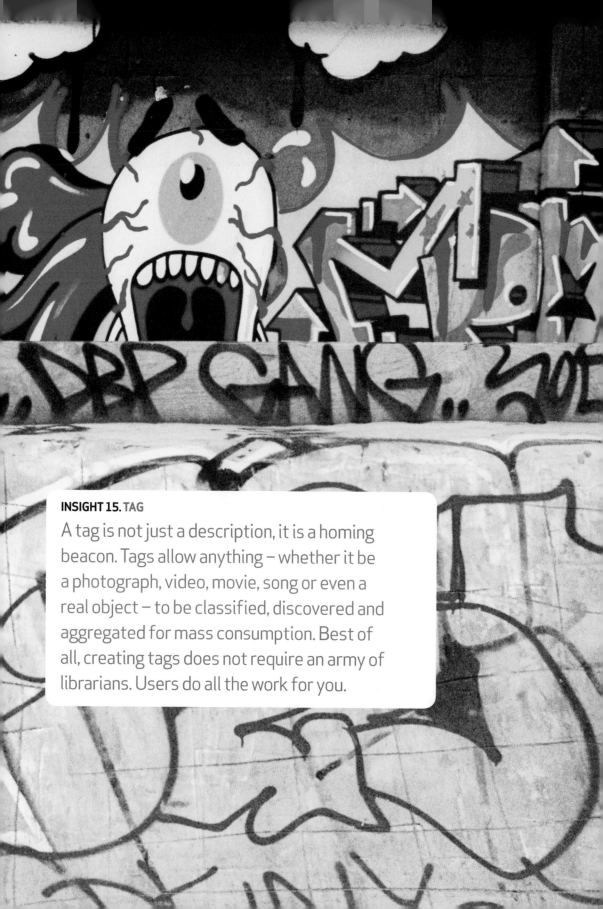

INSIGHT 15. TAG

A tag is not just a description, it is a homing beacon. Tags allow anything – whether it be a photograph, video, movie, song or even a real object – to be classified, discovered and aggregated for mass consumption. Best of all, creating tags does not require an army of librarians. Users do all the work for you.

FUN ⟩

16. SHIFT

MUST FOLLOW

One of my favourite theories as to why mobile content took off so quickly in Japan concerns the subway, which millions of Japanese people use every day for commuting. Too tightly jammed in to read a newspaper, passengers have just enough elbowroom to stare obsessively at the tiny screens on their mobile phones. Whether mobile dating, watching television or reading downloaded manga comics, more people in Japan access the Internet from mobile devices than from desktop computers.

This is not only happening in Japan; all over the world our lives are becoming busier and more nomadic. No one really has time for appointment viewing, so we grab snacks of entertainment – a quick video, a casual game, a few songs – when we can, wherever we happen to be.

People are starting to think in terms of entertainment commitment. Retailers describe certain types of merchandise as being considered purchases as opposed to impulse buys. For instance, you might buy a new wallet on a whim, but you would probably think twice about purchasing a new sofa.

Entertainment is the same: it is easy to agree to watch something that will entertain you for a moment, but committing to an entire movie or TV show seems like a weightier decision – or is it?

とう
東
Tō

しんにほんば

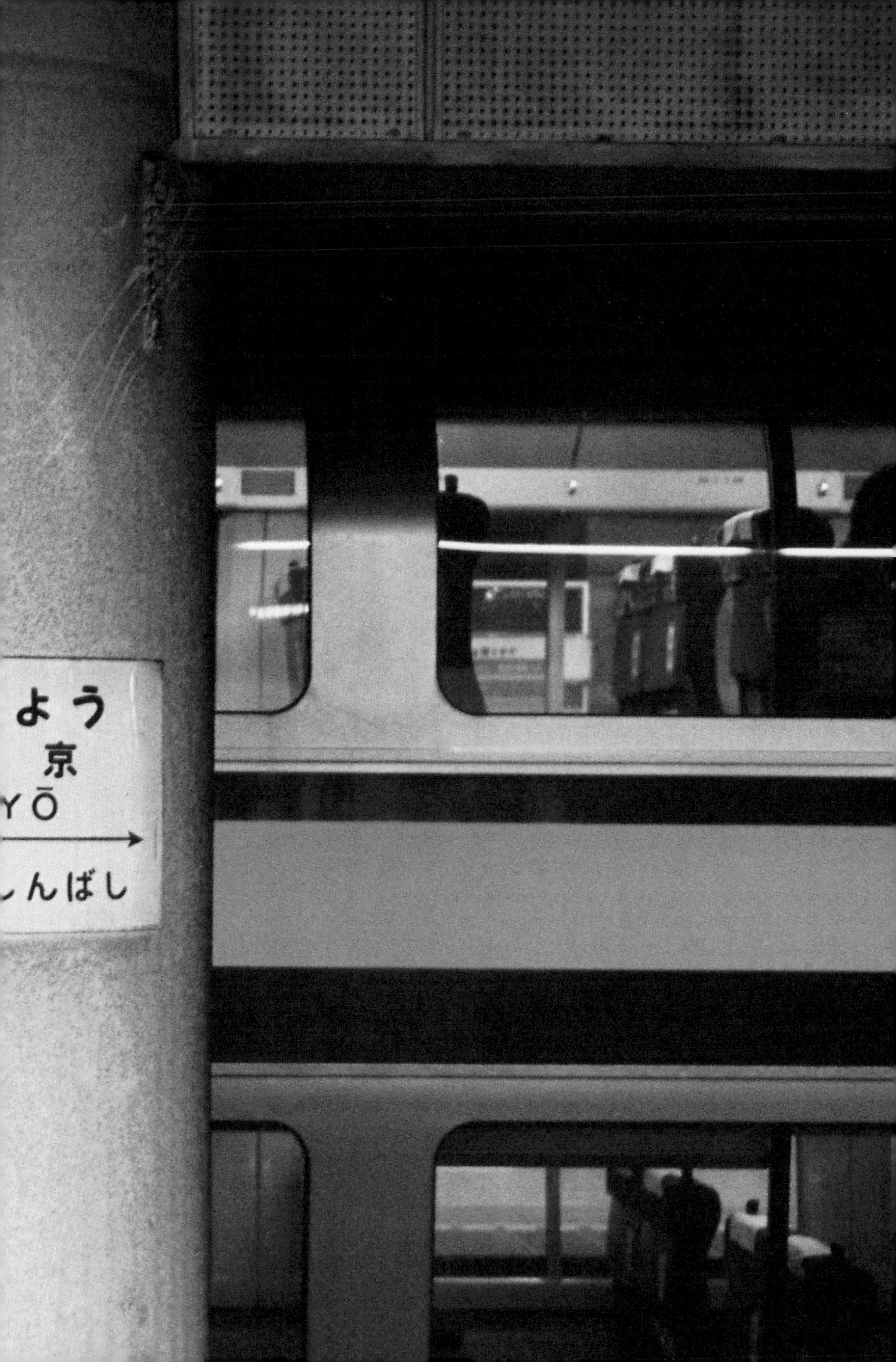
よう
京
YŌ
しんばし

While it is not entirely true to say that the VCR changed the consumer entertainment business (in fact, its initial impact was to create a billion dollar market in adult movies and exercise tapes), it did introduce a new way in which audiences could experience television: Time-shifting.

Time-shifting meant that the viewer was no longer locked into the programming schedule of broadcasters. For the few who could figure out how to use their VCR timers, suddenly it was possible to watch your favourite TV show without being at home when it was broadcast. Consumer electronics manufacturers experimented with simplifying buttons and commands, but it wasn't until the next generation of Digital Video Recorders (DVR), such as the TiVo or the Sky+ box, that the average TV-watching household discovered the power of Time-shifting.

The DVR changed the experience of watching television forever. An entire series of a TV show could be automatically recorded, to be watched at your leisure, and the box was even clever enough to fill any remaining space on its hard drive with other shows that it thought you might like, based on your programme preferences. Viewers are no longer limited to traditional satellite- or cable-delivered TV shows; the latest generation of DVRs are now connected to the Web, bringing the world of Internet content to living-room televisions and making the experience of consuming online entertainment indistinguishable from that of broadcast television.

Appointment television hasn't entirely died out, of course; big sports matches and reality TV shows, where knowing the result beforehand ruins the suspense, still manage to pull together large simultaneous audiences.

However, once time was under the control of audiences, space was the next to change.

In a 2009 interview with US broadcast journalist Charlie Rose, the CEO of Google Eric Schmidt talked about the limitations of today's media devices. He envisioned a world where powerful mobile devices made it possible to do everything that we do today, whether it be reading books or watching television, in very high quality. However, more importantly, those networks of the future would also have a memory – something, according to Schmidt, that does not happen now:

'When I turn on the television, it shows the same shows that I saw yesterday and I watch them and it doesn't know that I watched them yesterday. What a foolish television. Why is it not smarter?'

You can imagine the future scenario: you are at home watching the latest big budget action film on your vast, wall-mounted screen with surround-sound speakers. Your mobile device alerts you to the fact that your taxi has arrived to take you to the airport. You hit the pause button and leave the house. Once you are settled in the taxi, you turn on your portable device and keep watching from where you had left off. Later on, when you take your seat on the aeroplane, another network-connected screen awaits you; once again you can press play and continue watching. This whole seamless process can be thought of as Screen-shifting.

Screen-shifting, made possible by network-streamed content, means that your entertainment experiences can travel with you, literally jumping from screen to screen.

It is not unlike the convenience of being able to access your email wherever there is an Internet connection, without having to go back to the office.

Forget this madness of trying to create special content for different-sized screens – great entertainment shouldn't be limited by format. In the future, our format distinctions – mobile, CD, DVD, Blue Ray – will not exist. A movie will simply be a piece of software capable of scaling in resolution automatically to suit the screen you are watching it on, be it a small, hand-held device, or a home cinema in high definition.

INSIGHT 16. SHIFT

In the future, entertainment platforms will have a memory. Whether we are watching a movie or reading an eBook – our devices will record and learn from our actions, allowing us to easily shift our media consumption to whatever screens are available to us at the time.

Screen-shifting

CREATION

IS

COMBINATION

 By all accounts, music DJs were the first to use the phrase 'mashup' when describing the process of taking a vocal track from one song and combining it with the instrumental track of another. Before long, everything from seventies movie soundtracks to eighties rock classics were being sampled, modified and remixed into startling new creations. The results varied in quality, but were occasionally eerily inspired. The real pleasure of listening to a well-executed mashup is the sensation of being constantly pulled between two familiar tracks played simultaneously, while also hearing the dissonant resonance of an entirely new sound.

But mashups are no longer the domain of professionals – now that everything is digital, virtually anyone can take music and video and combine them in new and inventive ways. Just how powerful these tools are in the hands of the new generation struck me in the early days of YouTube when, browsing through the popular lists, I kept finding references to Amimated Musc Videos (AMVs).

These usually include a variety of content sourced from Japanese manga or the Cartoon Network, and integrated to pop music. The skill of making a great AMV lies not only in synchronizing the action to the music, but also in blending a variety of striking content sources. The creators of the most popular AMVs tend to be about twelve or thirteen.

Entertainment content was not the only candidate for a little mashing up; at the same time, web platforms would soon demonstrate the power of combining data as well as content.

The first generation of websites were irreverently referred to by scornful programmers as 'brochure-ware'. Although often attractively designed, they lacked vitality and served as little more than electronic brochures. Web platforms were different; first appearing as social networking services such as MySpace, Google Earth, Blogger, Flickr and Facebook, they combined the functionality of software with the ability to openly share data with other websites around the world.

Sharing was the key. Looking up a map was one thing, but far more interesting was the ability to create your own maps which combined photos from one website with hotel reviews from another site, and then share the results with your friends on other platforms.

This new spirit of web collaboration was facilitated by web platforms' publication of their Application Protocol Interfaces (APIs), which opened a back door that allowed other developers to gain access to the inner workings of a website for their own purposes. Although this might seem like the commercial equivalent of offering a set of house keys to anyone who asks, it is actually a great way to exploit the network effects of mass adoption. To use an entertainment analogy, the process is similar to when a band independently releases the instrumental track of one of their songs as an incentive for other people to creatively experiment with their music.

Forward thinking platforms that allowed developers access to their APIs included Google Maps, the blog network Typepad and the photo-sharing network Flickr. Among successful early mashups were the real-estate application HousingMaps and GawkerStalker, which allowed fans to post sightings of their favourite celebrities. Another popular mashup enabled fans of 'American Idol' to zoom in on each of the contestants' hometowns.

APIs create benefits for both developers and service providers. Developers can integrate data into niche applications that otherwise wouldn't warrant the cost of building the appropriate mapping software or collating millions of blog or photo entries. Equally, by sharing data, web infrastructure providers ensure that their service becomes more embedded in the overall media landscape.

We are used to the modern reality of media multitasking. You read the newspaper while listening to the radio, as the television flickers in the background your mobile beeps with messages and probably a web-connected computer stands not too far away. In a networked media environment, this meshing of media can now take place on a single screen, either as a Cluster or a Blend. Audiences in the future will be able to selectively programme their consumption to incorporate multiple entertainment experiences.

Many of us are familiar with the 'picture in picture' feature on a TV set, which allows you, for example, to keep an eye on a sports event in one corner of the screen while watching another programme. In the future, it is not too difficult to imagine this system being used to displaying a wider variety of information – a video feed of a movie, a share price counter and a text box showing scene-by-scene comments from your friends and favourite critics, or recommendations of films and music based on what you are currently watching.

This visual technique is known as Clustering, and it is a visual technique frequently used on financial news channels such as Bloomberg to present a high density of information on a single screen. The more sophisticated version of Clustering is Blending, in which consumers can atomize and overlay entertainment and data services to create entirely new forms of content. For example, a teenage boy might use this method to construct an entertainment feed which consists of the following:

The top thirty videos watched by the first two degrees of his social network during the last week.

Combined with a soundtrack of his favourite music, with two minutes extracted from each song and played in order of the closest fit in pitch and tempo.

Overlaid with superimposed text of the most-used adjectives that appear as comments on his individual profile.

Once created, he could then share this dynamic feed with everyone in his social network – quite possibly eventually generating a viral hit that is bigger than the original content that was mashed up in its inception.

We are increasingly moving towards a culture in which the major language of communication and representation is not words but rich media. Mashups will become part of the syntax through which audiences of the future will both consume and communicate. Media consumers today are far too voracious to be content with a single source of information, and when multitasking for content is so natural, overlaying several data inputs is inevitable.

INSIGHT 17. MASH

The age of shrink-wrap is over. Content is no longer hermetically sealed but open to being remixed, reissued and then re-distributed. But the new mashup culture is not just limited to entertainment. The most powerful web platforms of tomorrow will be those that open their data and applications for integration into a myriad of other online services, in the hope of becoming the new industry standard.

Clustering

Blending

FACT IS A FUNCTION OF

18. IMMERSE

FICTION

In 1966, a young Nolan Bushnell was walking through the University of Utah when he saw 'Spacewar', one of the first coin-operated video games. It must have left a lasting impression, as Bushnell soon started his own game company. He called it Atari, a word taken from the traditional Japanese board game 'Go'. The title of Bushnell's first game was simply 'Pong'. The production values of 'Pong' were not particularly impressive, but this did not matter; Bushnell's rudimentary coin-op was more than just a hit, it started a cultural revolution.

Games are still big business, and therefore run to large budgets. Requiring extensive teams of programmers and artists, as well as massive marketing campaigns: high-profile games now rival Hollywood films in terms of financial outlay. Fortunately, there is a considerable upside: today's games are no longer solitary affairs but multiplayer playgrounds, in which millions of simultaneous users pay either monthly subscription fees or real money for virtual items.

Multiplayer games are especially popular in China, where the relatively dull fare on conventional television means that, for young people, connecting with others through online game arenas is not just another form of entertainment – it is the only form of entertainment. Cybercafés in Beijing are filled with kids of all ages clicking away furiously on keyboards in the gloom. It may not be particularly high-tech, but it is about the most fun that you can legally have for a couple of yuan.

What makes online games so addictive has little to do with their visuals, gameplay or even the fabulous worlds and characters dreamed up by their designers; it's all about the activity of playing against real people. This blurs the lines between fact and fiction, as if sharing the vision of an alternate world with someone else makes it a more concrete and more immersive experience.

For its 2006 One Big Weekend concert, the BBC pulled out all the stops. The music line-up was impressive: Franz Ferdinand, Snow Patrol and Pink played, while thousands of fans danced and waved fluorescent glow-sticks on a private island, complete with tents and a gigantic stage. There was just one strange thing about the event: many people weren't actually there – not in a physical sense at least. The BBC held an exact mirror of their real-world concert in Scotland in a game called 'Second Life' – an online, 3-D virtual world that is entirely built and owned by its players. There were 30,000 people at One Big Weekend in Dundee and at least 6,000 participating in the virtual simulation of the concert.

The virtual world of 'Second Life' was one of the first computer simulations to create a self-sustaining universe, in which users created the world's objects, shaped the rules of behaviour and contributed to an internal economy. Ownership is an intrinsic feature of reality. When I spoke to Philip Rosedale, the founder of 'Second Life', he explained that he had drawn inspiration from an essay written by the Peruvian economist Hernando de Soto on the economics of land. De Soto believed that the most important characteristic of capitalism was the protection of property rights in a formal system that clearly recorded ownership and transactions. This resulted in greater trust, more efficient exchanges and ultimately stronger economic growth. Rosedale adapted this concept within 'Second Life', promoting the view that any object created online should belong to its creator, who has the power to assign, share or sell the item. Perhaps even more than graphic realism, knowing that what you have made actually belongs to you is a powerful tenet in your ability to trust the validity of a simulation.

Virtual ownership is more than simply a clever marketing tool; user-generated content is also part of the future of interactive entertainment. As games became multiplayer applications, they were forced to become more complex in order to keep up with the collective logic of millions of people. Continually inventing new characters, quests and game items became both expensive and difficult. This is why the innovative American computer game designer Will Wright, inventor of 'Sim City', the ground-breaking game that allowed players to create their own cities, enabled users to populate the universe of his latest game, 'Spore', with their own creations. By assigning the complex task of world building to users, Wright not only reduced the cost of assembling a game universe, he gave players the opportunity to take ownership of the very things they might imagine.

In many ways, the next generation of games won't resemble games at all. They will be more of an overlay to our own experience of reality. Weaving around real-world events and people, and subverting our own technology, they will seduce us into believing that we are not playing, but constantly living a life of adventure.

Some of these games will be casual: a game of chess with someone sitting in the café across from you, a soccer match among economy and first class on an aeroplane, or even a tennis match between two opponents on either sides of the planet. Others will be more integrated and pervasive; in the next few years, we will start to see entirely new genres of immersive entertainment that take full advantage of the possibilities of networked personal data.

Imagine a game environment that can not only integrate real world events and news feeds, but also draw on your own archives of photos, videos and connections to deliver personalized experiences that could lead some users into a state of game-induced paranoia.

In the future, games will invade our lives.

INSIGHT 18. IMMERSE

Games have evolved from simple tests of skill, to complex simulations. They offer an interface that attracts millions of other players around the world. The next stop is total integration – when gaming platforms begin to incorporate our personal information and co-opt devices from the real world. Soon we will stop playing with games. They will start playing with us.

YOUR ONLY
POWER IS
KNOWING
YOU NOW
HAVE NONE

POW

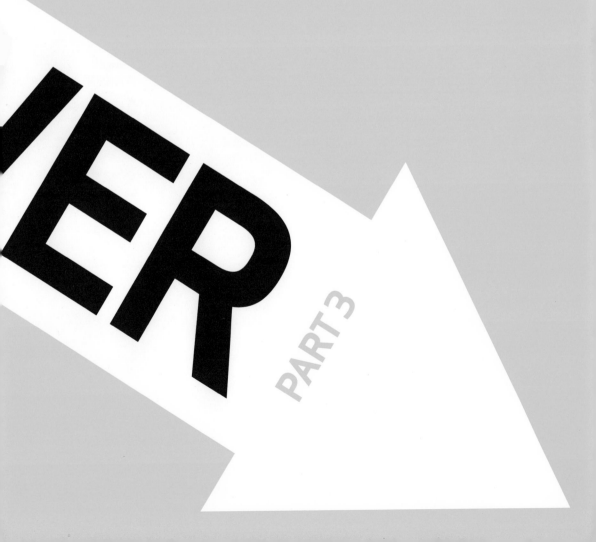

THE PACKAGE IS MORE PRECIOUS

THAN THE

PRIZE

19. META

No piece of content exists in a vacuum. Every movie, TV show, song or book is made up not only of its original content, but also of what other people have to say about it. This 'content about content' is incredibly valuable, because it allows people to discover and make decisions about what media they want to consume. Another word for this surrounding content is Metadata and, in a way, it is nothing new.

When Frederick Leypoldt arrived in the United States from Germany in the late nineteenth century, he started working as a bookseller. He soon realized that he had a problem. For his book business to be more efficient, he not only needed a supply of good books, but also information about the books themselves. For example, he needed to know which books had been published, when they had been published and who had published them. Finding this information difficult to obtain, Leypoldt decided to do something about it himself.

In 1870, Leypoldt issued the first edition of the *Annual American Catalogue*, a publication that would eventually become *Books in Print*. In 1878, Leypoldt's company was acquired by Richard Rogers Bowker, and together Leypoldt and Bowker created more reference sources such as *Literary Marketplace* and *Ulrich's International Periodicals Directory*. The book information market exploded. As more books were published around the world, the importance of information about the books increased. In the late sixties, the International Standard Book Number (ISBN) was created as a way of keeping track of the millions of books in print. The company that Leypoldt and Bowker had created, now called R. R. Bowker, became the official US ISBN agency, responsible for tracking and providing information for the book industry.

Many years later, in 1994, a former investment banker called Jeff Bezos decided to create the world's biggest retailer of books without actually having a physical bookstore. He named the company Amazon and projected it to be entirely web-based. To achieve this, Bezos required more than just a large inventory of books – he needed the ultimate database of everything in print. Initially, R. R. Bowker gave him what he needed, but as Amazon grew in size and popularity and expanded the number of products it carried to include CDs, DVDs and other consumer goods, something interesting happened. While R. R. Bowker simply continued adding to their basic reference library of published book titles, Amazon continually enhanced its data feeds, adding cover images, tables of contents, indexes and sample material of the books it featured, as well as user-generated content such as reviews, consumption data and wishlists for a wide range of products.

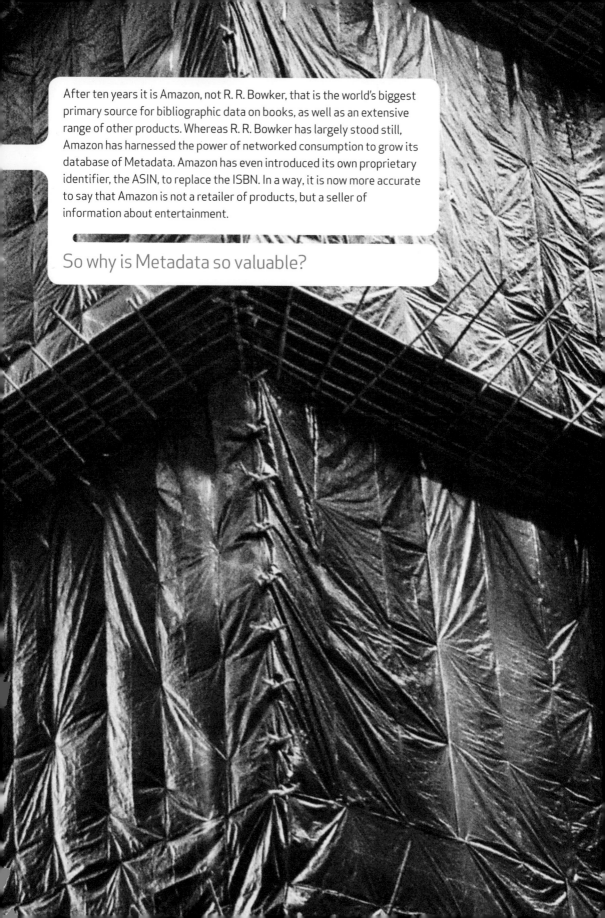

After ten years it is Amazon, not R. R. Bowker, that is the world's biggest primary source for bibliographic data on books, as well as an extensive range of other products. Whereas R. R. Bowker has largely stood still, Amazon has harnessed the power of networked consumption to grow its database of Metadata. Amazon has even introduced its own proprietary identifier, the ASIN, to replace the ISBN. In a way, it is now more accurate to say that Amazon is not a retailer of products, but a seller of information about entertainment.

So why is Metadata so valuable?

Content Core

Data Layer

Data Sleeve

What once applied solely to books can now be appropriated to all kinds of media. The greater the number of people that consume a piece of content, the more information is created about that material. This information, which can be a review, rating or even a statistic showing that someone has watched a particular film at a specific time, forms a kind of data layer – a second skin of information, or what I like to call a Sleeve.

A Sleeve can include all kinds of information about content: ratings, tags, comments, reviews, related fan works and records of other people who have consumed it. The original content core – say a movie like *Casablanca* – may remain unchanged, but year after year the cumulative effect of people watching, discussing and analysing the film gradually increases the amount of content in its Sleeve.

The Sleeve is important because it is what makes content visible on the Web. Taking even the most simple example of searching for something on Google, the more that people create content about content, the more paths develop to that original piece of media, and consequently the greater the chance that it will be accessed by someone who is looking for it. In this way, everything inside a content Sleeve provides a navigational aid towards the original content.

The use of Metadata leads to a curious outcome. After all, can you think of any other instances of economic goods that increase in value the more frequently they are consumed? The more traces people leave after consuming entertainment, the easier it becomes to find. The value here, in economic terms, is tangible; ease of discovery lowers the cost to the consumer seeking to be entertained. There is also a broader information dimension at play; the community response to media is, like the extras on a DVD, increasingly part of the work itself.

Naturally, this raises an interesting question for media companies. How do you retail entertainment products in such a way that encourages audiences to help you grow the information value of what you are providing? Or put more simply, how can you motivate your customers to help grow your Sleeve?

To answer this fully, we need to look at the future of aggregation.

INSIGHT 19. META

More valuable than content is the stuff that surrounds it. Reviews, recommendations and ratings are not only a by-product of consumption, they also make media more visible and, in doing so, increase its underlying market demand.

PAY PER

20.SLICE

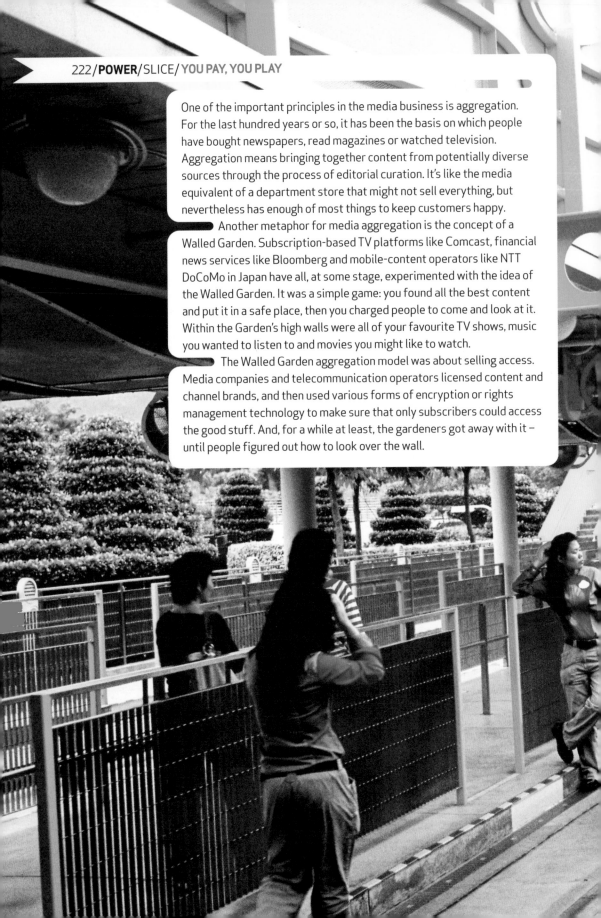

One of the important principles in the media business is aggregation. For the last hundred years or so, it has been the basis on which people have bought newspapers, read magazines or watched television. Aggregation means bringing together content from potentially diverse sources through the process of editorial curation. It's like the media equivalent of a department store that might not sell everything, but nevertheless has enough of most things to keep customers happy.

Another metaphor for media aggregation is the concept of a Walled Garden. Subscription-based TV platforms like Comcast, financial news services like Bloomberg and mobile-content operators like NTT DoCoMo in Japan have all, at some stage, experimented with the idea of the Walled Garden. It was a simple game: you found all the best content and put it in a safe place, then you charged people to come and look at it. Within the Garden's high walls were all of your favourite TV shows, music you wanted to listen to and movies you might like to watch.

The Walled Garden aggregation model was about selling access. Media companies and telecommunication operators licensed content and channel brands, and then used various forms of encryption or rights management technology to make sure that only subscribers could access the good stuff. And, for a while at least, the gardeners got away with it – until people figured out how to look over the wall.

Ask someone why the Berlin Wall fell and you will rarely get a simple answer. They may mention capitalism, pop culture, democracy, student rallies or a combination of factors. But whatever the reason, the message was clear: once people on one side had realized that life was elsewhere, it was only a matter of time.

The arrival of the Internet had a similar impact. Audiences suddenly started to discover that there was a whole universe of content available to them. Some of it was new and made by other users, but much was the same as the stuff that they had been paying a premium to access for years. This was not good news for the Walled Garden model.

On 28 May, 2009, the board of directors of Time Warner approved the spin-off of AOL, bringing to an end what had once been hailed as the historic merger of one of the world's largest media companies with a subscription-based website. The rise and fall of AOL provides an insight into why Walled Gardens no longer work as they once did.

AOL began in the early eighties as a venture called Control Video Corporation (CVC), which allowed owners of the early Atari video game consoles to download games from a private server at a cost of US$1 per game. It was an idea that was ahead of its time, but difficulties with manufacturing and management very nearly left the company bankrupt. As the decade wore on, the company changed strategy to focus on providing online services for the new generation of home personal computers such as the Commodore 64, Apple II and the IBM PC, eventually rebranding itself as America Online.

When Steve Case took control of the company in the early nineties, he positioned the business as a service for people who were new to computers. AOL offered its users access to a varied yet controlled range of content, initially for an hourly fee, but in 1996 it started to charge a flat rate of US$19.99 per month. Within three years of setting up this model, AOL's user base grew to 10 million people, before peaking in the early 2000s with almost 30 million customers. These massive subscription revenues underwrote AOL's ability in 2000 to merge with the traditional media giant Time Warner. However, in a short space of time, the value of AOL dropped drastically, forcing AOL Time Warner to report a loss of US$99 billion in 2002, which was then the largest loss ever in US corporate history. Not surprisingly, its management thought that it was an appropriate time to drop the name AOL from the company brand. So what happened?

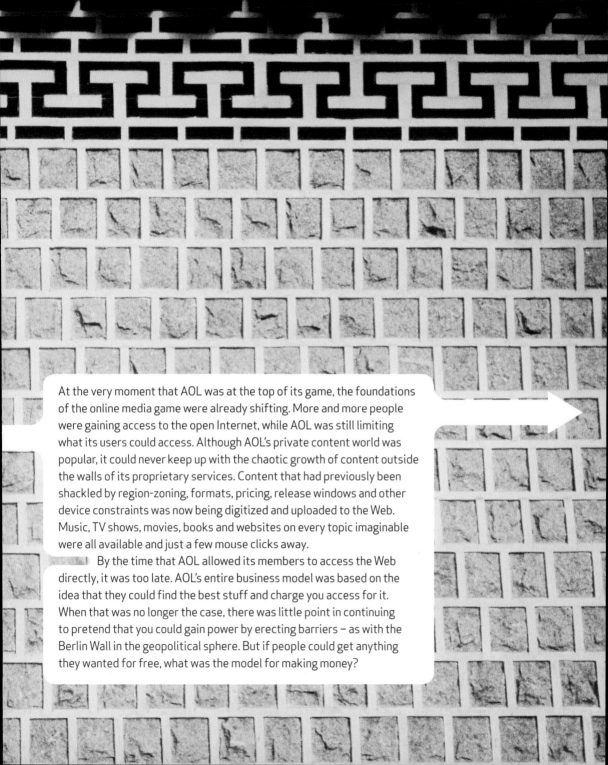

At the very moment that AOL was at the top of its game, the foundations of the online media game were already shifting. More and more people were gaining access to the open Internet, while AOL was still limiting what its users could access. Although AOL's private content world was popular, it could never keep up with the chaotic growth of content outside the walls of its proprietary services. Content that had previously been shackled by region-zoning, formats, pricing, release windows and other device constraints was now being digitized and uploaded to the Web. Music, TV shows, movies, books and websites on every topic imaginable were all available and just a few mouse clicks away.

By the time that AOL allowed its members to access the Web directly, it was too late. AOL's entire business model was based on the idea that they could find the best stuff and charge you access for it. When that was no longer the case, there was little point in continuing to pretend that you could gain power by erecting barriers – as with the Berlin Wall in the geopolitical sphere. But if people could get anything they wanted for free, what was the model for making money?

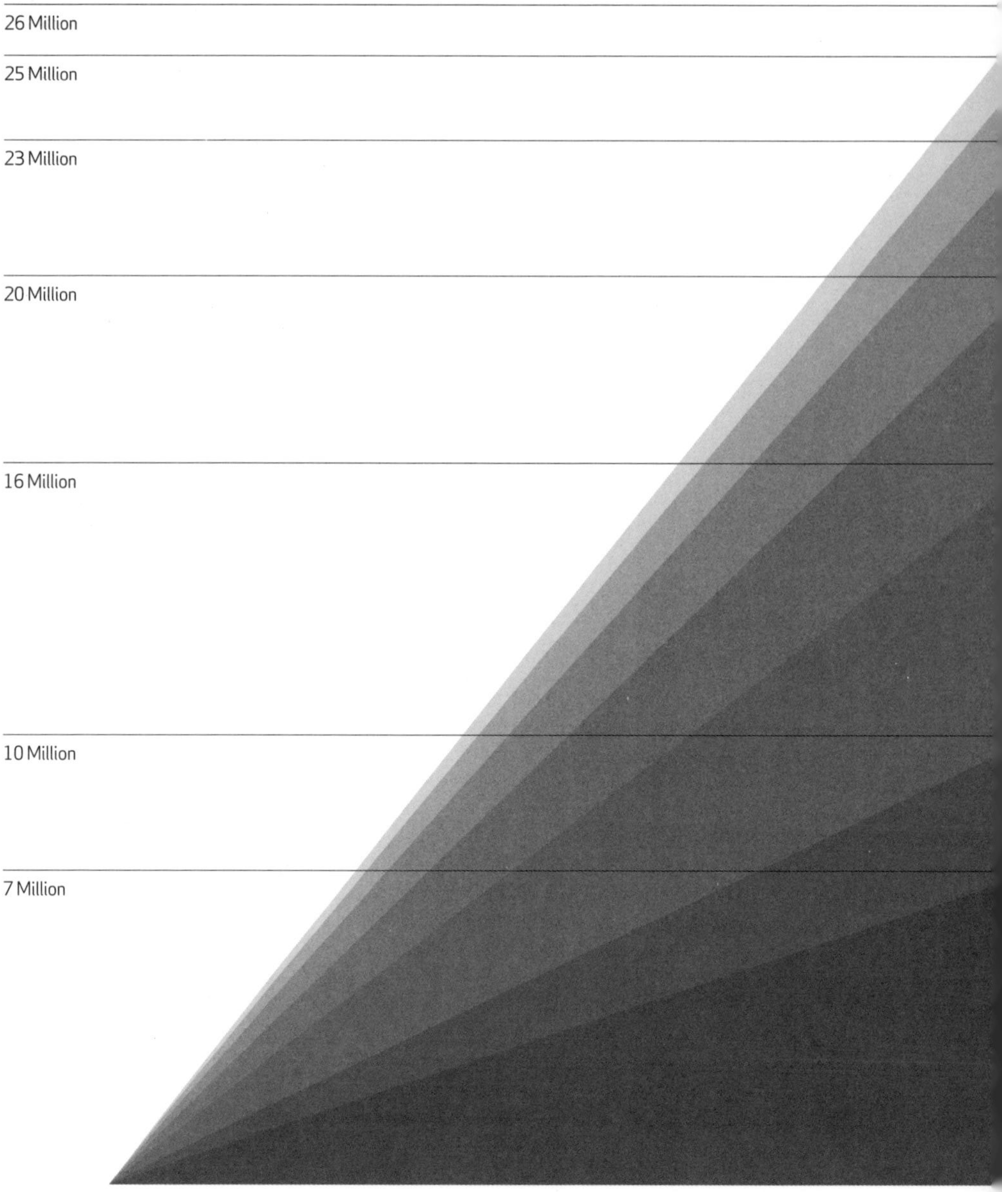

26 Million

25 Million

23 Million

20 Million

16 Million

10 Million

7 Million

Year
2002
2003
2004
2005
2006
2007
2008

With enough charisma to turn a mundane product launch into the Second Coming, Apple founder Steve Jobs is nothing if not persuasive. Even so, few people took him seriously when he announced that the company had plans to sell digital music online in conjunction with their newly launched MP3 music players.

The accepted wisdom was that people either bought CDs in shops or they accessed music for free online – there was no market in between. Besides, the original iPod was expensive and only compatible with Apple computers, which meant that the planned iTunes store had only a tiny potential market share. Ironically, it was probably a combination of all of these misconceptions that allowed Jobs to seduce the record labels into allowing him to sell their tracks for a minimal fee.

A few years later, with the iPod established as a social pheno-menon and Jobs cutting deals with Hollywood Studios to offer movie downloads along with music, his detractors had to eat their words. Jobs had been right – this really was the new way to sell content. iTunes was successful because it tapped into a fresh model of aggregating enter-tainment: organization. This system is about information; it's what you can offer when you have collected enough 'content about content' to provide a meaningful context for media. This context is the magic ingredient that helps people to make informed decisions about the entertainment they want to consume.

Although consumers could easily get music for free on the Internet, they were happy to pay a small amount for it so that:

- Music tracks were provided to an acceptable standard, with integrated album art as a feature.
- The more you used the service, the more accurate the music recommendations became.
- Music tracks were supplemented by a wealth of professional and consumer reviews, and cross-referenced to similar artists and genres.
- You could share your playlists with your friends, who could then immediately purchase your music choices and add them to their libraries.
- Apple made it easy to organize and rate your music library, whether on your computer or portable music device.

Like Amazon, Apple was not in the business of selling entertainment products – it was a savvy aggregator selling information about entertainment. Apple's innovations paved the way towards making aggregation-based businesses work in the future. AOL was proof that it was not enough just to offer interesting content – in order for people to want to rely on a media company for their entertainment experiences, it had to be able to add value to material through organizing and referencing content.

In a sense, the next generation of media aggregators to emerge over the coming years will not be aggregators at all. Aggregation itself is a kind of hoarding: businesses monopolize the best content and only offer people access to it if they pay enough money. The new approach that will be taken by media companies is closer to Slicing.

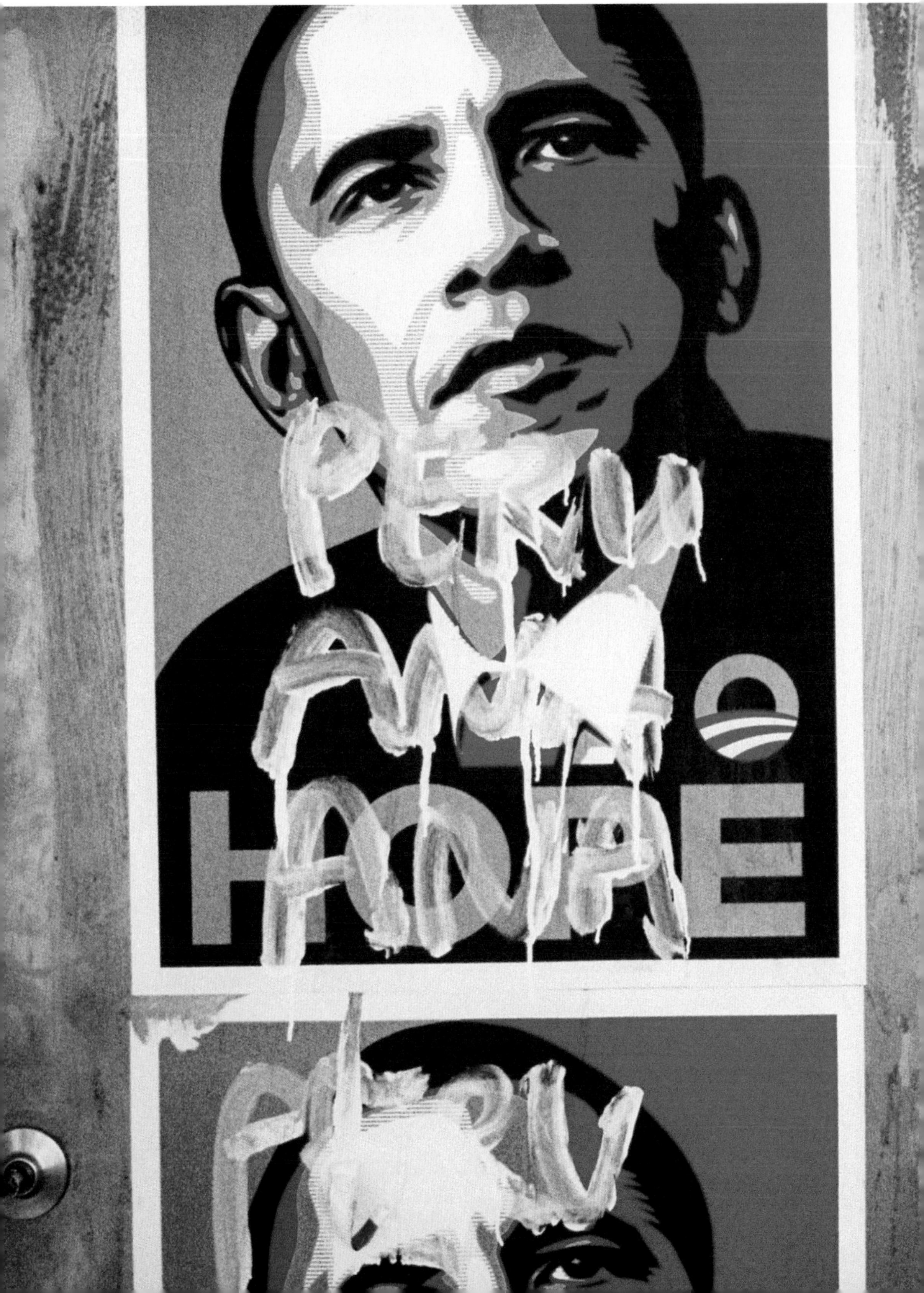

Social networks are a vital source of information for media discovery. There is a wealth of data that is implicit to any Audience Network, ranging from what fans might say about a particular song, to raw consumption data like the number of times someone has listened to a particular track. By drawing insights from this data, entertainment slicers are able to assemble content in a highly individual fashion.

In the old days, radio networks conducted thousands of listener surveys to come up with the best possible selection of music that would appeal to the widest number of people. These days, making decisions for millions on the basis of a statistical sample of a few thousand seems downright archaic, especially when compared to the ability of companies like Apple to draw insights from hundreds of millions of iTunes users, and inform the media selections of audiences on a personalized basis.

However, Slicing is more than just a clever set of media recommendations; in a world of almost infinite on-demand content choices, entertainment slicers will offer audiences curated media experiences that combine content, reviews, ratings, promotional material and fans themselves. More than just content, they will develop an entire community based upon the enormous wealth of entertainment content offered by the Internet.

The critical point is that it will no longer be enough for media companies to provide access to content. Discovery, recommendations, related features and the ability to connect with other like-minded entertainment consumers will play a much bigger role in winning the battle for media time than just making content available.

For audiences, the real value is no longer content but context.

INSIGHT 20. SLICE

In a world where you can get any piece of content for free, media companies will no longer be able to rely on Walled Gardens for survival. Instead, aggregators of the future will create value by understanding the individual preferences of customers and creating personalized slices of entertainment for them.

21. PLATFORM

If you were to head twenty-five nautical miles offshore from the coast of the Caspian Sea, you would find something rather unusual: a floating city.

Called the Neft Daslari (the Oil Rocks), it was built in 1947 off the coast of Azerbaijan. The Neft Daslari was the world's first oil platform and is still the largest, with more than 200 km of streets, various shops, a school and a library, all built on piles of dirt and landfill. The 5,000 inhabitants of the complex work in shifts – a week on the platform, followed by a week on the shore. Neft Daslari exists for one purpose – to supply oil – and yet it is so much more. It is a fully functioning ecosystem, which is capable of supporting multiple objectives, inhabitants and businesses. In addition, it is a useful metaphor for thinking about how we might engage with media in the future. After all, when is an entertainment product more than just content? When it is also a platform.

Platform is a word that you are going to hear more often in relation to the media industry. So far, we have explored the idea that content has an information dimension greater than itself, and that in the future aggregators will use this to organize entertainment experiences for consumers. But content brands also have a bigger future in store.

Something that Hollywood has known for decades is that the most successful content brands are more than just songs, movies or TV shows – they are franchises in their own right. It won't be long before that calls for something a little grander than a mere website.

The most valuable factor within a successful piece of entertainment is not the creative material itself but the content brand.

Hollywood is well aware of this fact. Making movies is an expensive business. According to the Motion Picture Association of America (MPAA), in 2007 it cost Hollywood studios an average of US$70.8 million to produce a film and US$35.9 million to market it, adding up to a US$106.6 million total price tag.

The more you spend on making a movie and encouraging people to watch it, the more important it is that you can extend the value of the content brand. When you have a strong content brand, it can be used to sell all kinds of related products: across multiple sequels or seasons, or tied in with merchandise, marketing promotions and spin-offs. In the past, commercializing these opportunities was a complex process, involving multiple countries, partners and retail channels. Digital distribution is starting to simplify that practice, although it is simultaneously increasing competition. The importance of being able to manage brand franchises in the movie business has meant that in recent years new players have been able to enter the field, such as Marvel Comics. With a strong stable of popular comic hero brands, Marvel was well placed to both independently finance and market big budget movies such as *Iron Man* and *The Hulk* rather than simply licensing their content to a traditional Hollywood Studio.

Marketing has long played a pivotal role in the ultimate success of a movie release. Since the early days of the Internet, a website has featured in the marketing campaign of most movies. Primitive versions of such websites were fairly basic, with trailers, wallpaper downloads and some information about the plot, the cast and the production. In the foreseeable future, promotional movie websites will gradually transform into fully fledged entertainment platforms, merging content with environments in which audiences can connect through their experiences.

Some platforms will be dedicated to a single brand franchise – for example, a cartoon series like 'The Simpsons', or a movie series like *Star Wars* – while others will be wider, encompassing an entire genre of programming such as science fiction or sports. These genre-based platforms will replace what we used to think of as channels on TV networks.

Nevertheless, these platforms will have a number of common attributes:

MICRO TRANSACTIONS

Micro transactions with a low value but occurring at high frequency will allow content creators to merchandise a range of related products, including virtual items, music, fan clubs, personalized apparel, events and toys.

TARGETED ADVERTISING

The interactive environments of platforms will enable brands to capture their target markets' attention in a context that is relevant to the content.

USER-GENERATED CONTENT

Platforms will provide a rallying point for consumers to contribute or link to their own material which references, remixes or responds to the original content.

DATA BY DEFAULT

Data about patterns of consumption and habits will be collected automatically and used to tailor entertainment experiences to the audience and suggest new ones that they might enjoy.

FEEDBACK

Feedback is the magic ingredient of interaction. Platforms will reflect what users say and do. When you tell someone how often a piece of content was viewed, commented on, made a favourite or linked to, you might be surprised by how much this encourages them to create and consume more content.

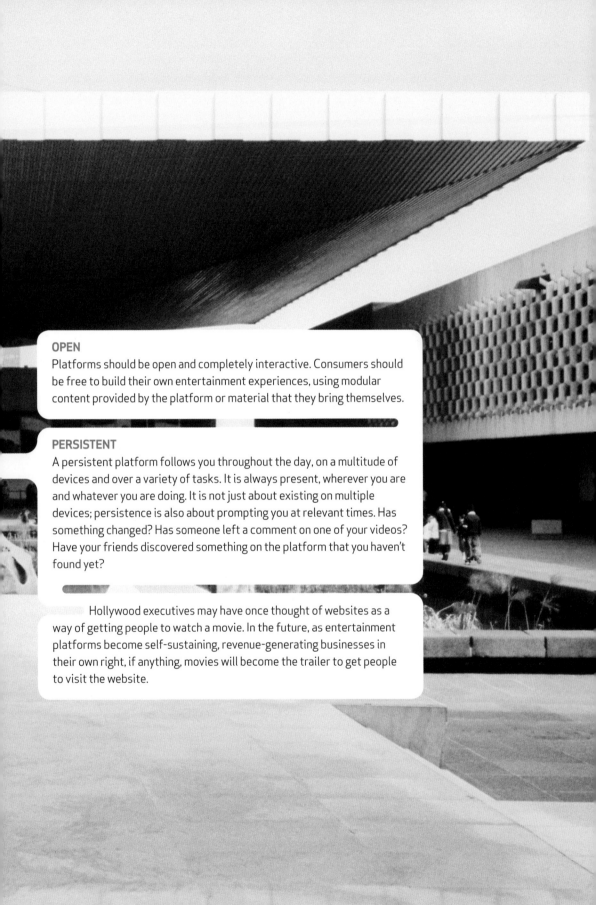

OPEN

Platforms should be open and completely interactive. Consumers should be free to build their own entertainment experiences, using modular content provided by the platform or material that they bring themselves.

PERSISTENT

A persistent platform follows you throughout the day, on a multitude of devices and over a variety of tasks. It is always present, wherever you are and whatever you are doing. It is not just about existing on multiple devices; persistence is also about prompting you at relevant times. Has something changed? Has someone left a comment on one of your videos? Have your friends discovered something on the platform that you haven't found yet?

Hollywood executives may have once thought of websites as a way of getting people to watch a movie. In the future, as entertainment platforms become self-sustaining, revenue-generating businesses in their own right, if anything, movies will become the trailer to get people to visit the website.

Tokyu Hands is not like any other department store. Although it started life in Japan as a do-it-yourself store specializing in craft and project supplies, it soon expanded to become a diverse emporium of the weird and wonderful. I found myself wandering through the isles of the Shibuya outlet in Tokyo with Tim O'Reilly, the media commentator and publisher.

As we walked past shelves of unusual stationery, toys, and miniature appliances, I thought about the talk I had seen O'Reilly give some days before. Since the mid-nineties, he had been considering the significance of open-source software. In the early eighties, IBM believed that the market was all about hardware, so it signed the software rights to their nascent operating systems to Microsoft. However, Microsoft realized early on that software was in fact the key to the future, and the company was able to build a huge business around it. In O'Reilly's view, the same thing happened with the Internet.

O'Reilly explained that, over the last few years, the very nature of websites has been changing. They are moving away from merely offering content and towards operating more like software, signalling the rise of the Internet as a platform. Applications on the Internet actually work better as more people use them: every time that someone makes a link from one site to another they contribute to the intelligence of the Google search engine; the more people join Facebook the better it works in linking people together; the more users buy and sell on eBay the better it works as a marketplace; the more people listen to music on iTunes the smarter the service gets at making recommendations and creating playlists for its users.

For all the talk of openness, O'Reilly realized that the natural direction in which this is taking us is towards the creation of new monopolies. Collective intelligence applications improve as greater numbers of consumers use them, creating true economies of scale. The companies that are better at harnessing this collective intelligence will take over, making it harder for new companies to break in. It is, in other words, a winner-takes-all game.

This was a salutary lesson. Media companies were once protected from competition by a combination of high capital costs, regulation and geographically restricted markets; in the future, consolidation and monopolization will still be inevitable outcomes, but this time they will emerge as a result of scale and critical mass.

INSIGHT 21. PLATFORM

The next step for entertainment brands goes beyond mere merchandise. Box office revenues will eventually pale in comparison with the commercial opportunities offered by sophisticated online platforms. These platforms will allow fans to engage and participate in engineered worlds that more closely resemble multiplayer games than traditional movies or TV shows.

TALL

TOLD

22. ENGAGE

TALES ➤

TRUE ➤

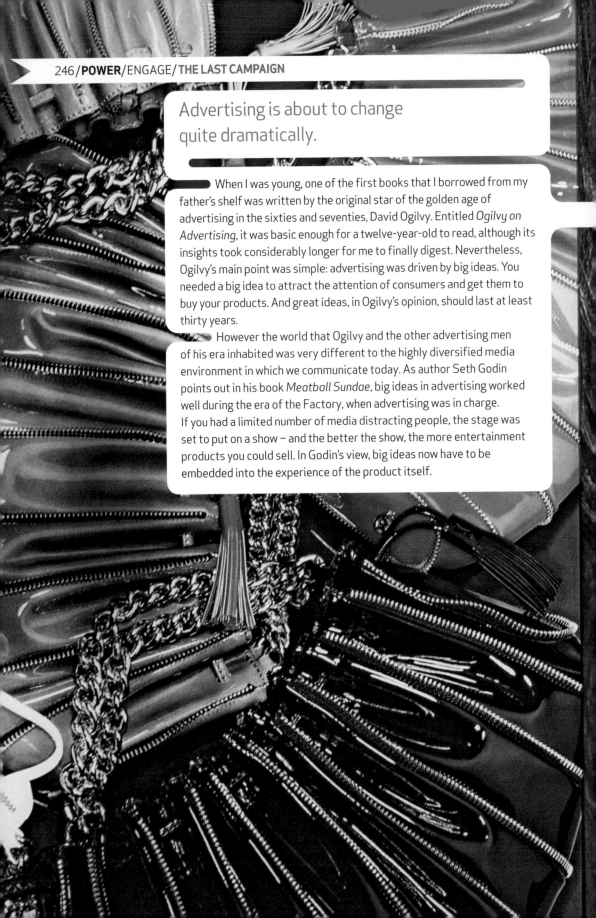

Advertising is about to change quite dramatically.

When I was young, one of the first books that I borrowed from my father's shelf was written by the original star of the golden age of advertising in the sixties and seventies, David Ogilvy. Entitled *Ogilvy on Advertising*, it was basic enough for a twelve-year-old to read, although its insights took considerably longer for me to finally digest. Nevertheless, Ogilvy's main point was simple: advertising was driven by big ideas. You needed a big idea to attract the attention of consumers and get them to buy your products. And great ideas, in Ogilvy's opinion, should last at least thirty years.

However the world that Ogilvy and the other advertising men of his era inhabited was very different to the highly diversified media environment in which we communicate today. As author Seth Godin points out in his book *Meatball Sundae*, big ideas in advertising worked well during the era of the Factory, when advertising was in charge. If you had a limited number of media distracting people, the stage was set to put on a show – and the better the show, the more entertainment products you could sell. In Godin's view, big ideas now have to be embedded into the experience of the product itself.

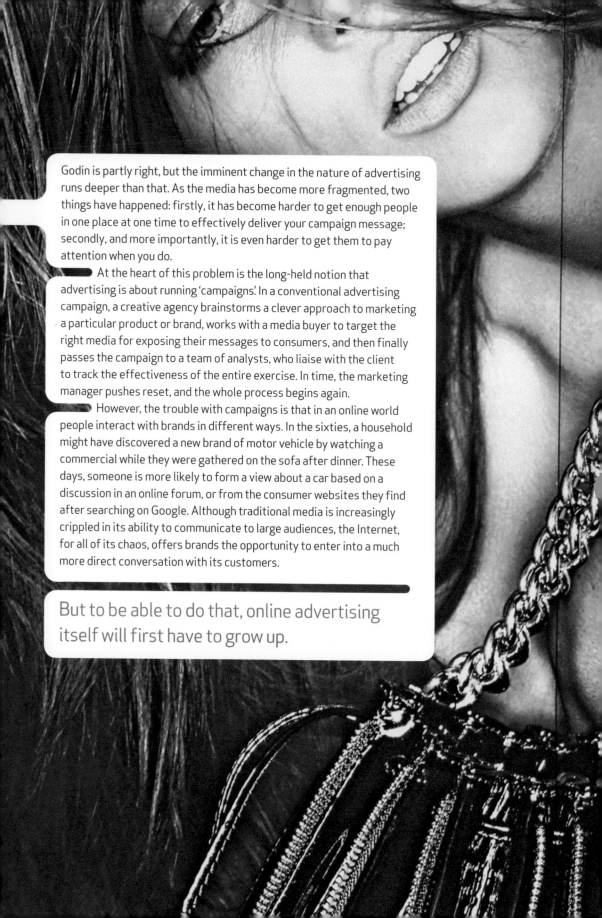

Godin is partly right, but the imminent change in the nature of advertising runs deeper than that. As the media has become more fragmented, two things have happened: firstly, it has become harder to get enough people in one place at one time to effectively deliver your campaign message; secondly, and more importantly, it is even harder to get them to pay attention when you do.

At the heart of this problem is the long-held notion that advertising is about running 'campaigns'. In a conventional advertising campaign, a creative agency brainstorms a clever approach to marketing a particular product or brand, works with a media buyer to target the right media for exposing their messages to consumers, and then finally passes the campaign to a team of analysts, who liaise with the client to track the effectiveness of the entire exercise. In time, the marketing manager pushes reset, and the whole process begins again.

However, the trouble with campaigns is that in an online world people interact with brands in different ways. In the sixties, a household might have discovered a new brand of motor vehicle by watching a commercial while they were gathered on the sofa after dinner. These days, someone is more likely to form a view about a car based on a discussion in an online forum, or from the consumer websites they find after searching on Google. Although traditional media is increasingly crippled in its ability to communicate to large audiences, the Internet, for all of its chaos, offers brands the opportunity to enter into a much more direct conversation with its customers.

But to be able to do that, online advertising itself will first have to grow up.

In the early days of online advertising, publishers needed a language to explain to advertisers what they were selling. So, in the same way as cars were once referred to as 'horseless carriages' and escalators 'moving staircases', the language of online media was phrased in reference to the world it actually replaced. Online ads were sold by a negotiated CPM rate, or cost per thousand. CPM was a ratio that was originally developed for traditional media, where you calculated the cost of a campaign according to the number of people it reached; to work out the final budget for your advertising spend, the key data to track was audience impressions.

I like to think of this state of affairs as Flatland. In Flatland, media is consumed in a linear fashion, and advertising is inserted into the flow of consumption in classic 'interruption' style. You may no longer hear a voiceover saying 'we interrupt this programme to bring you a message from our sponsors', but the intent is still there. Whether in commercial breaks on television, full-page ads in a magazine or thirty-second radio spots – Flatland sold advertising as an insertion, measuring the scale of the campaign through the impressions of its audience.

Impressions

Flatland

However, the problem with choosing impressions as the basis for selling online advertising is that the Internet works in an entirely different way to traditional media. Whereas everyone who watched an episode of 'Desperate Housewives' would see a Ford ad at the same time, on the Internet people viewed content at different times and in different places. Every time someone visited a web page, it counted as another impression. The more popular your content, the more impressions you had to sell.

Consider this simple example. If you purchased 50,000 impressions on a low traffic website, you could be fairly sure that anyone visiting the site would see your ad every time they logged on. But lets say you bought the same campaign on a website that received a million impressions a month, the chance of your campaign appearing to anyone visiting the site would now be relatively low. So, while a TV station could estimate with certainty just how much inventory it had to sell – on the Web, publishers were perennially trying to deal with the challenge of having an almost limitless inventory with an ever-decreasing impact.

In actual fact, if you spend time looking at content on the Internet that refers to brands, you will notice something very interesting. If you type into Google any number of brands you will discover that only a very small proportion of the content in the search results derives from a current advertising campaign. Depending on the brand, you will find a multitude of other information, including reviews written by consumers, fan websites, media reports and stories, communities of interest, Wikipedia entries on the origin of the brand, retail product listings and thousands of other odd bits and pieces. The sum of this all can be eclectic and chaotic, but it represents the totality of conversations that consumers are having about products and is far more influential in the long run than any one particular advertisement. On the Web, advertising campaigns simply don't exist like they do in broadcasting or print media.

So how will the brands of the future take advantage of this shift? If there is an opposite to Flatland, it is what I call Loopworld. Loopworld is based on the notion that the Internet is an enormous, open forum for discussion which gives the opportunity for brands and consumers to engage in a cycle of communication that benefits both parties. The feedback loop could be a simple process of consumers providing details about their lifestyle and habits, and brands responding with products and ideas that match their aspirations. Or it could be as complex as consumers actually creating their own content as a way of participating in the universe of their favourite brands.

If the yardstick of success in Flatland is whether or not someone has seen an ad, in Loopworld the measure is engagement. This occurs when consumers leave something of themselves with a brand. It could be by generating content, making recommendations to friends, sharing information about their preferences or simply indicating that you know they are paying attention to you. As anyone who has been to an anger-management class would know, getting people to listen requires more than shouting – you have to change tactics.

True engagement demands more than clever targeting and a cost-effective customer acquisition campaign; it requires the ability to tell a good story.

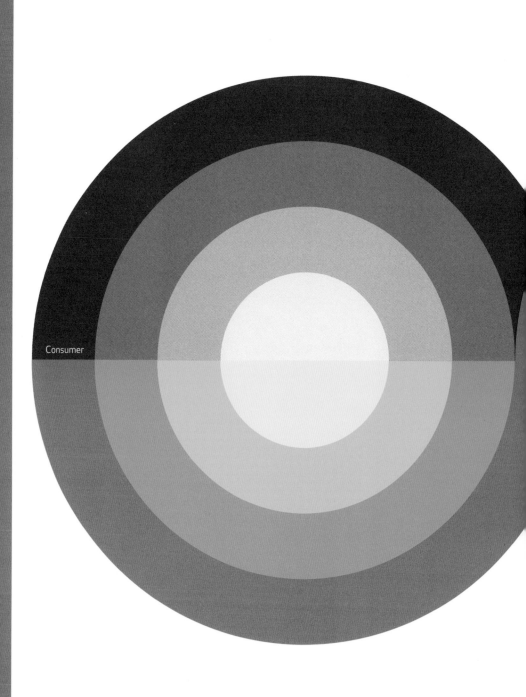

Consumer

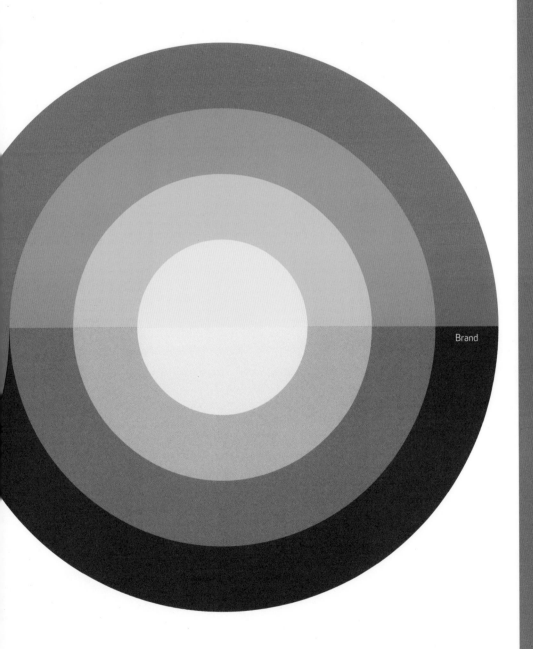

Brand

Brands engage consumers through telling stories.

There are a handful of brands I love: Leica cameras, Moleskine notebooks, Mont Blanc pens, Lucchese cowboy boots and Persol sunglasses. It is, I admit, an odd list, which may tell you more about myself than I would like, but the point is that all of these brands have great stories behind them – their history, their founders, their values and how they see the world. Most of these stories are probably apocryphal, but I don't mind – I want to believe them. By learning more about the stories that surround a brand, I shape my own impressions of their products and also what they mean to me in my own life and experiences.

Fortunately, the Web is the perfect environment for both creating and sharing brand mythologies – far more so than a thirty-second ad break. Brands not only have the opportunity to build rich websites that entertain and educate consumers about what they do but, more importantly, they can also participate in the fragmented conversations that are taking place about them. Search on Facebook and you will already find pages about brands where people contribute photos, stories, videos and reviews. Some of these were created by marketers, but most were originated by consumers themselves.

What this means is that brands have to start thinking like media companies. Not only because they need to create content that builds on their mythologies, but also because they are facing exactly the same challenge: audiences are now so fragmented that the only way for them to achieve mass awareness is for their message to be compelling enough for consumers to do the distribution for you. This is more than branded content; in a world increasingly fixated on authenticity, artificial product placement just won't cut it. In fact, it may well work against you.

The future of entertainment is not advertising – the future of advertising is entertainment.

INSIGHT 22. ENGAGE

The future of advertising does not lie in
big, complex online campaigns. The Web is
a powerful medium for telling stories. The
challenge for marketers will be to manipulate
digital platforms to create and sustain their
brand mythologies. As consumers become
smarter at eluding marketing, it will not be
sufficient merely to invent better looking
advertisements around content. Advertising
will need to become the content.

23. DISRUPT

IS TO CHANGE IT

I was never much of a surfer, but my father, a young English immigrant in Australia during the sixties, was an enthusiastic convert and I spent countless summers floating out in the ocean with him. This is when I learned that catching waves is quite an art. If you start paddling too early, you can miss the rising crest that carries you to the shore; however, if you start too late, it can wash right over you.

One of the hardest things to do for anyone who runs a company is to ensure they are positioned for that next big wave, which carries the latest trend. As well as the possibility of not being adequately prepared, it is easy to do too much too soon, when it is simply too early to be trying to change the market. And that is the most difficult question of all. Knowing about future opportunities is one thing, but the real issues concern predicting how soon they will arrive, what impact they will have when they do, and how much of your resources you need to devote to chasing them right now.

There are no easy answers to this, but in my opinion there are three main waves you need to worry about.

The first is *technology*.

During the first Internet boom, many start-ups spent millions developing cutting-edge content-management tools, which only a few years later would be more or less free as part of weblog publishing systems. Similarly, early video content and virtual-world ventures in the late nineties floundered because very few consumers were equipped with the high-speed broadband connections that were necessary to use such websites. A heartbeat later, and the situation had changed. Now billions of videos are watched every month by consumers online, and virtual worlds in Asia make millions in profits.

Sometimes there is a significant advantage in being first – you have a chance to build an early majority of users, establish your brand as the leader in the space and have first pick at commercial partnerships, gain further investment or consider a trade sale. But there is always a cost, and in most situations that means paying a premium for developing cutting-edge technology which may require supporting infrastructure, and systems that either do not yet exist or are financially prohibitive. Of course, if you wait too long for your particular technology to mature and become generally available, you also stand to lose much of your competitive advantage over more established players who often struggle with innovative Research & Development projects.

Technology   Behaviour   Business

Innovation Waves

That second wave is *behaviour*.

To really understand the impact of future technology, you have to think like an anthropologist. How people behave holds more significance than what new technology might allow them to do. Technologists have a bad habit of creating quirky solutions that are no longer popular (such as designing Super Audio CDs at a time when consumers were more interested in experimenting with low-fidelity, portable music). Behaviour is complex, and varies dramatically between cultures. Some ideas, such as virtual merchandise and multiplayer gaming, were easy to transplant from South Korea to China but required significant modifications to work elsewhere in the West. Observing patterns in consumer behaviour is more than just waiting for a critical mass of people to start doing something; it's about identifying trends that have the potential to disrupt existing ways of consuming media, doing business or sharing information. Often that means understanding the things that people do, even if these actions generate no obvious revenue at that moment in time.

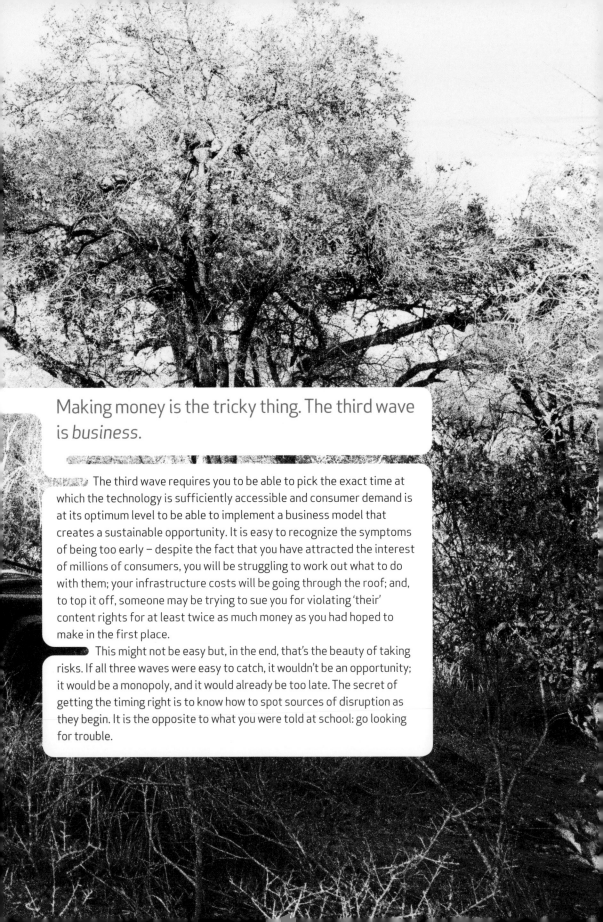

Making money is the tricky thing. The third wave is *business*.

The third wave requires you to be able to pick the exact time at which the technology is sufficiently accessible and consumer demand is at its optimum level to be able to implement a business model that creates a sustainable opportunity. It is easy to recognize the symptoms of being too early – despite the fact that you have attracted the interest of millions of consumers, you will be struggling to work out what to do with them; your infrastructure costs will be going through the roof; and, to top it off, someone may be trying to sue you for violating 'their' content rights for at least twice as much money as you had hoped to make in the first place.

This might not be easy but, in the end, that's the beauty of taking risks. If all three waves were easy to catch, it wouldn't be an opportunity; it would be a monopoly, and it would already be too late. The secret of getting the timing right is to know how to spot sources of disruption as they begin. It is the opposite to what you were told at school: go looking for trouble.

If there is one four-letter word that strikes fear into the hearts of most media executives it is this: *free*.

The biggest source of disruption in the media industry at the moment and for some time to come is the fact that consumers expect to be able to consume the vast majority of their entertainment content without paying for it. The signs are everywhere; despite the fact that 1.4 billion units of recorded music were sold digitally in 2007 (Nielsen Soundscan), an equivalent amount was traded every single month for free on peer-to-peer networks. The vast majority of China's 200 million web-users have never paid for music and, even the ones who do, benefit merchants who have probably pirated the CD. In South Korea, a market with 40-megabit download speeds, the Korean Film Council estimates that the average Korean web-user downloads 54.4 movies a year, decimating the DVD industry. DVD revenues in South Korea have dropped from a high of US$673 million in 2002 to only US$285 million in 2008.

Naturally, the initial response of the world's major entertainment companies when consumers started gravitating to free content was to threaten, cajole and sue. When that didn't work, they changed tack to invest, partner and redeploy. In recent times, all the major record labels have joined forces with MySpace to launch MySpace Music, a spin-off which makes streaming music available for free to the MySpace community, with plans to make money from ticket sales, merchandise and advertising. Hulu, a joint venture between two US network television rivals NBC and Fox, has initiated a similarly disruptive strategy to counter free video on the Web. Hulu now makes its prime-time TV shows available for free online and is expanding internationally.

Free content is not a death sentence. If anything, it has become an example of how disruptive consumer behaviour can, over time, shift even the most fossilized of media business models. Here are a few more scenarios in which the entertainment industry might be forced to respond to consumer disruptions in the years to come:

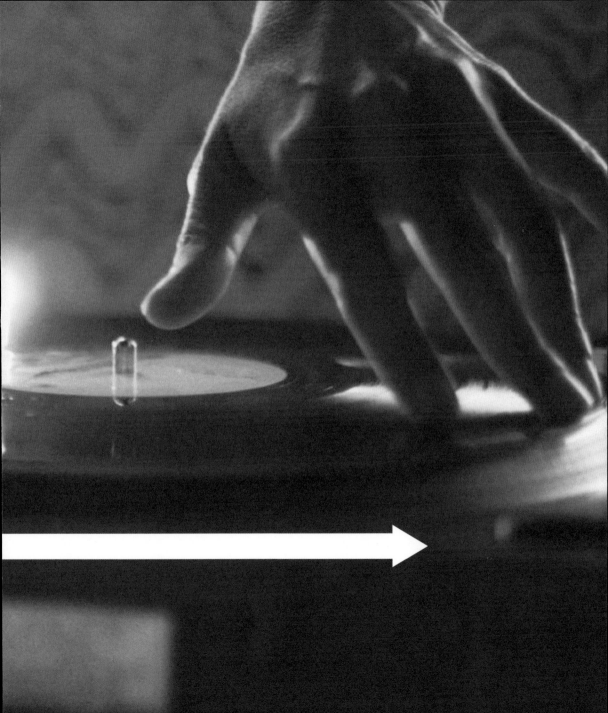

All distribution windows collapse and TV networks stream everything for free, simultaneously with broadcasting.

Broadcast channels are designed to drive viewers to their web platforms rather than vice versa.

Consumption patterns fragment across multiple devices, but intelligent content networks record what you were watching, allowing you to pick up from where you left off.

Studios produce more content for the Web than they do for traditional broadcast media.

All advertising goes digital and is delivered to individuals on a targeted, personalized basis.

Popular content brands develop their own platforms for merchandise, communities and transactions.

Subscription television focuses on smart aggregation and organization rather than simply providing access to content.

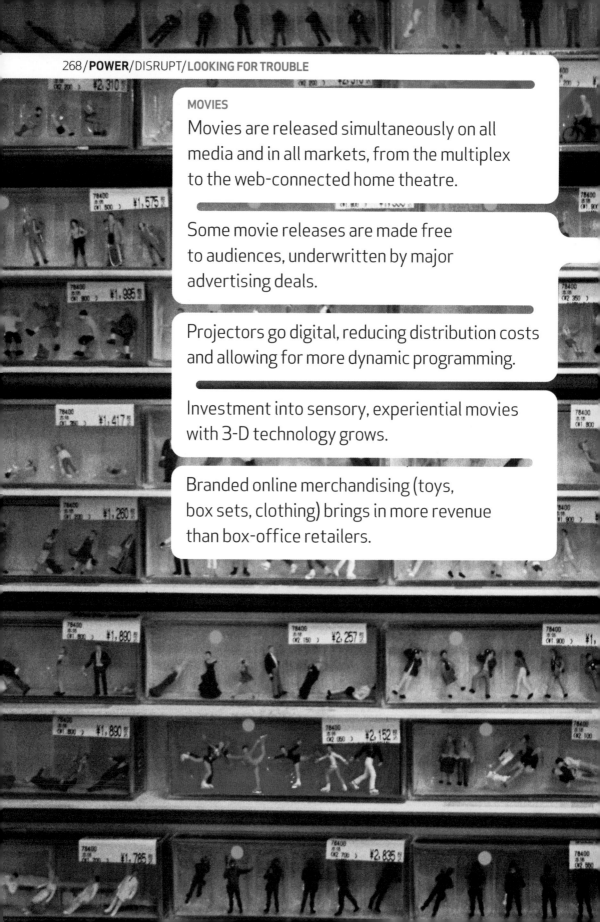

MOVIES

Movies are released simultaneously on all media and in all markets, from the multiplex to the web-connected home theatre.

Some movie releases are made free to audiences, underwritten by major advertising deals.

Projectors go digital, reducing distribution costs and allowing for more dynamic programming.

Investment into sensory, experiential movies with 3-D technology grows.

Branded online merchandising (toys, box sets, clothing) brings in more revenue than box-office retailers.

MUSIC

The world's entire library of recorded music is available for free on any device.

Music business models rely on a combination of advertising, merchandising and events.

Subscription-based models dwindle and increasingly fade away.

Personalized streaming on mobile devices and in cars becomes mainstream.

Digital radio takes longer to reach the mass-market than expected, and innovation is driven by the Web and mobile devices.

A five-way competition breaks out between TV brands, radio broadcasters, music labels, social communities and music hardware companies to win the attention of consumers.

GAMES

Network multiplayer games dominate, and eventually overtake teenage media time from other media.

Free business models (with revenues from advertising and virtual items) replace subscriptions.

Games become a key entry point for music and product launches for the youth sector, and attract more advertising and sponsorship.

Casual gaming booms, driven by mobile usage and the spread of location-based technology.

The focus moves from creating more complex consoles to accessories, extensions and immersive controllers.

More games become movies than movies become games.

The important thing to remember about all of this is that change is as unpredictable as it is inevitable. There is a new generation of media consumers growing up right now who have never known a world without the Internet, and accordingly have never endured the same constraints on consumption, creation and distribution of content that many of us have. Their frame of reference is completely alien to us, but will become increasingly influential as they discover new ways to engage with entertainment and each other.

Old business models, partnership agreements, legal precedents and organization structures will not provide an adequate defence against the massive shifts in consumer behaviour. The changes will not be easy, but it certainly won't be boring. As one of my favourite playwrights, Tom Stoppard, points out in *Arcadia*: 'It's the best possible time to be alive, when almost everything you thought you knew is wrong.' In the end, irrespective of what you believe the future of media to be, one thing is for certain:

As interesting as it is when things change, the real magic happens when people do.

INSIGHT 23. DISRUPT

Sometimes the best way to win a game is to question why you are even playing it. The rules that govern industries are rarely made in advance – they evolve in periods of rapid change until eventually they themselves become the restraints on innovation. But there is one thing you can be sure of: when consumer behaviour changes, sooner or later business must follow. As to where things go next, the answers lie in front of you. The future is already here, you just need to know where to look.

The photos in this book were taken on my travels with my trusty Leica M6 loaded up with 35mm film. It is a strange kind of irony. The future may be digital, but my heart is still firmly analogue.

RESET Yesterday the World changed, now it's your turn

PLAY You see children playing; I see future soldiers of the Revolution

POWER Your only power is knowing you now have none

1. **REVOLUTION** Change Always Appears Incremental Until it's Too Late

2. **FACTORY** Mass Produced Media Must Make Way for Media Produced by the Masses

3. **MEDIAJACK** You Can't Stop the Music

4. **NETWORK** Everyone is Connected

5. **UBIQUITY** Anywhere, Anything, Anytime

6. **WHERE** Where is the New When

7. **CROWD** We are Smarter Together

8. **SOCIAL** Who You Know is What You Know

9. **DISCOVERY** We Will Watch What Others Will See

10. **VIRAL** One Becomes Many

11. **AVATAR** We Are What We Want Others to See

12. **LIFECAST** We Desire to Live Each Others Lives

13. **PULSE** Life = Change

14. **AUTHENTIC** We Want to Believe

15. **TAG** To Name is to Find

16. **SHIFT** Fun Must Follow

17. **MASH** Creation is Combination

18. **IMMERSE** Fact is a Function of Fiction

19. **META** The Package is More Precious than the Prize

20. **SLICE** Pay Per Skew

21. **PLATFORM** More is More

22. **ENGAGE** Tall Tales Told True

23. **DISRUPT** To Win the Game is to Change it

INDEX

3G 70
Abrams, J. J. 175
Adamic, Lada 139
advertising 248–67
Agfa 154
aggregation 222, 228–32
Amazon 121, 124, 216–17
American Express 120
'American Idol' 198
AMV (Animated Music Video) 197
Annenberg, Walter 118
AOL 224–7
API (Application Protocol Interface) 199
Apple 90, 228–9, 231
ARPANET 66–8
Atari 224
audience networks 28, 31, 58–9, 61–3, 98, 100, 124–5, 233
avatars 142–51
Backdorm Boys 24
Bell, Gordon 156, 161
Berners-Lee, Tim 68
Bezos, Jeff 216
Biofeed 168
BitTorrent 48, 53
Blackberry 72
blending 200–1, 203
Bloomberg 200, 222
Borges, Jorge Luis 178
Bowker, Richard Rogers 216–17
Boyd, Danah 114
Brand, Stewart 50
brands 234–6, 252–3
Buffet, Warren 40
Bush, Vannevar 156
Bushnell, Nolan 207
Case, Steve 224
CBS 125
CD, impact of, 45–6
China, new media in 20, 22–5, 207
cliff effect 32–3
Cloverfield 174
clustering 200–2
Clutrain Manifesto 174
Comcast 222
crowd intelligence 96–100
Cyworld 109, 148, 150
De Soto, Hernando 208
'Desperate Housewives' 48, 250
Dewey, Melvil 178
Deyo, Yaacov 106
Digg 98, 166, 169
Del.icio.us 98, 182
Digital Rights Management 48
Dunbar, Robin 109
DVR 189
Eastman, Gergoe 154
eBay 144, 242
eBooks 191

Euler, Leonhard 56, 58
Facebook 62, 106, 113, 199, 242, 254
factory model 36–41
Flickr 180–1, 199
Fox 27
Friendfeed 98
Friendster 148
Furong JieJie 24
games 207–10, 272
GawkerStalker 199
Geoweb 78, 82–7, 88, 90
Global Positioning System (GPS) 82–4
Gladwell, Malcolm 131
'Go' 207
Godin, Seth 246–7
Google 27, 60–2, 180, 190, 242, 247, 250
Google Earth 84–5, 90
Google Maps 199
GPS (Global Positioning System) 82–4
Granovetter, Mark 113
Guare, John 113
Hackers' Conference 50
hacking 47, 53
Hilton, Paris 174
Hollywood 53, 76, 228, 236, 238, 241
HousingMaps 199
Huberman, Bernardo 139
The Hulk 238
Hulu 27, 264
IBM 242
information cascades 100, 136
iPhone 90
iPod 48, 182, 228
Iron Man 238
ISBN (International Standard Book Number) 216–17
iTunes 48, 50, 90, 121, 233, 242
Jennicam 160
Jobs, Steve 228
JonasBrothers.tv 160
Kan, Justin 160
Kermack, William 130
'King of the World' 148
Königsberg (Kaliningrad), seven bridges of 56–8
Kutcher, Ashton 160
Lagerfeld, Karl 182
Last.fm 125
Leskovec, Jure 139
Levine, Rick 174
Leypoldt, Frederick 216
Library of Congress 181
Licklider, J. C. R. 66
Lifecasting 160–3
Locke, Christopher 174
Loopworld 250–3
McKendrick, Anderson Gray 130
Marvel Comics 238
mashups 199–201

media arbitrage 50–1
mediajacking 48, 53
Memex 157
metadata 216–18
Microsoft 242
Mixi 148
Mobagetown 148
Murdoch, Rupert 26, 27
MySpace 27, 62, 106, 113, 148, 199
MySpace Music 264
Nakamatsu, Yoshiro 45, 46
Napster 53
NBC 27
Neft Daslari 236
Netflix 121
Netscape Navigator 20, 68
News Corporation 27
Newton, Isaac 94, 100
Nintendo 144
NTT DoCoMo 222
O'Reilly, Tim 242
Ogilvy, David 246
packet-switching 66–8
PaiKe 88
peer-to-peer networks 51
personal video recorders 118
Polaroid 154
'Pong' 207
Qik 161
QQ 24, 25, 148, 150
Rekimoto, Jun 82
Ringley, Jennifer 160
Rose, Charlie 190
Rosedale, Philip 208
SARS 128
Sartre, Jean-Paul 118
Schmidt, Eric 190
screen-shifting 190–3
Searls, Doc 174
'Second Life' 148, 208
Shirky, Clay 178
'Sim City' 208
The Simpsons 118, 238
Sky+ 189
slicing 230–3
social networks 106–15
Sony Walkman 124
'Spacewar' 206
speed dating 106
'Spore' 208
Starbucks 90
Star Wars 238
Stoppard, Tom 274
Stumbleupon 98
super distribution 135, 138-9
Surowiecki, James 136
Sweeney, Anne 48
Tencent 25
Tianxian MeiMei 24

Time Warner 224
Tivo 118, 189
TV Guide 118
Twitter 98, 109, 160, 161
Typepad 199
ubiquitous networks 70–3, 74–9
VCR 189
virtual currencies 150
viruses 128–39
Vonnegut, Kurt 142
walled gardens 222–4
Watts, Duncan 130, 136
Weinberg, David 174
WiFi 70
Wii 144
Wikipedia 250
WiMax 70
'World of Warcraft' 144
Worshipful Company of Stationers and
Newspaper Makers 26
Wright, Will 208
Xiao Pang 24
YouKu.com 88
YouTube 27, 90, 138, 173, 174, 196

ABOUT THE AUTHOR

Mike Walsh is a leading authority and keynote speaker on the digital future. He is the CEO of the innovation research agency Tomorrow and has over a decade's experience in helping some of the world's leading companies and brands embrace new ideas. Mike previously ran Jupiter Research in Australia, and also held strategic roles at News Corporation in both the Australian and Asian markets.

AUTHOR'S ACKNOWLEDGEMENT

Futuretainment was art directed by Vince Frost and Quan Payne at Frost*Design. An internationally recognized and multi-award winning designer, Vince Frost is known for his innovative use of photographic images and striking typography. Formerly at Pentagram in the UK, Frost now runs his international design studio from Sydney, Australia.

Phaidon Press Limited
Regent's Wharf
All Saints Street
London N1 9PA

Phaidon Press Inc.
180 Varick Street
New York, NY 10014

www.phaidon.com

First published 2009
© 2009 Phaidon Press Limited

ISBN 978 0 7148 4875 4

A CIP catalogue record for this book
is available from the British Library.

Photographs by Mike Walsh
Designed by Frost*Design

Printed in China